To Judith M. Moss,
in recognition of
her understanding heart.

THE ART OF COMMUNICATION
A Self-Help Course in Basics

Dorothy Myers Reed

July 22, 1982

Books by Dorothy Myers Peed

*The Art of Communication: A Self-Help
Course in Basics*
America Is People and Ideas

THE ART OF COMMUNICATION

A Self-Help Course in Basics

Dorothy Myers Peed

An Exposition University Book

EXPOSITION PRESS   HICKSVILLE, NEW YORK

To

ROBERT BOVIE MYERS

Only that day dawns to which we are awake.
There is more day to dawn,
The sun is but a morning star.

THOREAU
From *WALDEN*, as inscribed
below the bust
of Thoreau in
the Hall of Fame.

I, at over forty, having spent a lifetime in doing abstract mathematics about the shape of things, suddenly saw my knowledge reach back over two million years and shine a searchlight into the history of man. And from that moment I was totally committed to thinking about what makes man what he is. . . . There is a gift above all others that makes man unique among the animals: his immense pleasure in pushing forward his own skill.

JACOB BRONOWSKI
From the film *The Ascent of Man*
as reported in
the *NATIONAL OBSERVER*
for January 26, 1974.

CONTENTS

Part Three
ENGLISH MECHANICS

PREFACE

Sammy Davis, Jr., was asked on a TV interview, whether or not he would like to see his children go into acting. His immediate reply was, "Only after they have obtained a college education. Fifteen years from now a good education will be a necessity."

Not everyone can get a college education. But everyone can make the most of his own abilities, can learn to respect his own thinking, relate it to his reading and writing, and improve his ability to communicate with others. That is why *The Art of Communication: A Self-Help Course in Basics* has been put together.

The term "put together" is factual, for this book is, quite literally, a distillation of teaching techniques which I received in my own schooling, and which I developed during my teaching career from junior high to junior college.

I believe three special factors influenced my career. First is a junior high education which included Latin in the eighth and ninth grades. At that time I was acquiring a Latin vocabulary at the same time I was learning the usage of English words. I recall, for instance, the ritual we had to go through to satisfy the Latin teacher when we "parsed a noun." What an out-of-date word and function today! We had to tell the kind, the gender, the number, the person, the case and the use of every noun. In the English class, it was not nouns but pronouns for which we needed to know the same answers if we were to use the correct form of a pronoun. Thus, the inclusion of Sidney J. Harris's column answering the question of the value to young people today of knowing Latin (page 129).

A second influence is described in "Recollections of Kitchen Table Conversations" during my high school, college, and early teaching years. These were conversations which, when combined with a Tufts College education, assured me of an interest in every discipline and gave me a feeling of belonging to a democracy where the individual counted and education was the liberator of the mind.

Somewhere in this book I have stated that my Space Age education began fifty years ago during these Kitchen Table Conversations. The spectrum of the twin stars which my astronomer friend was studying was, to her, equivalent to "fingerprints for identifying chemical elements in the stars," her grandfather and uncle's theory. Her personal history was combined with every subject for conversation (See Genealogy Chart, page 70). Thus, I was made ready, too, for our Bicentennial review of every square mile of land where Americans of all colors, races, creeds put their stamp on building a country.

My third influence grew out of this scrutiny of historic spots and people. It explains an influence which was so basic and so taken for granted that it needed to be pointed out on a map of Somerville, the city where I was born and educated. Somerville was known as "Charlestown Without the Neck" until 1842 when it was given the purely fanciful name of Somerville, a suburb of Boston. By whatever name, early history was made here, and to demonstrate to myself how very basic both my education and my surroundings were, I marked a map of the city using my junior high school location as the central point. I discovered that, from Western Junior High, it was: one-half mile to Powder House Park where the skirmish with the British in September, 1774, over gunpowder almost started the Revolution; one-half mile in another direction is the gravestone of a British soldier; one and one-third miles away is Paul Revere Park where he changed route and went through Medford to Lexington and Concord; the same distance in other directions are the homes of Oliver Tufts and Samuel Tufts, the decendant of whom "put a light on the Hill" in 1855 to found Tufts College; one and one-half miles away the first settler's house was located, he having come from

Plymouth to Charlestown; the same distance gets one to the Mystic River where early boat building went on; one and three-quarter miles takes one to Prospect Hill where the first flag of the United States colonies was raised on January 1, 1776; two miles away and just beyond Prospect Hill is the spot where a patriot, too old to run from the British, stayed to be shot; two miles in another direction the first telephone line was installed by Bell for Williams in whose electric shop he did his experimental work, and as a result owed Williams money—the line connected Williams's home with his shop in Boston; two and one-half miles in the same direction is Bunker Hill (the smoke of which battle Abigail Adams is said to have watched from her home south of Boston in Braintree); to commemorate another War, the first Civil War Memorial was erected in The Old Cemetery, which is land given for that purpose by Samuel Tufts—land for the first school in Somerville was also part of this land gift. On a lighter, more modern note, about half a mile in the opposite direction from the above is the MTA Carbarn, the same MTA of ballad fame.

As the years passed, immigrants from many countries made Somerville their home, for there were industries of all kinds and Boston was only three miles away.

From this base, then, and over a teaching career comes *The Art of Communication: A Self-Help Course in Basics* including the Language Basics which represent the foundation of education, and the People Basics which represent, nationwide, the struggle to be an individual who is free to make the most of himself.

From 1957 on, when I first began putting ideas of grammar and library study on paper, I was encouraged by a Miami professor, a Florida senator concerned about education, a colleague who shared my ideas, a department head who gave me freedom to work them out, many lecturers and educators who recognized value in my teaching approach.

Three adjectives from a national newspaper editor, now retired, gave me courage for the days when teaching grammar was almost forbidden. He wrote, "This is obviously the result of interested, original, and experienced thinking."

PART ONE
INTRODUCTION

INTRODUCTORY COMMENTS

Dorothy,

I'm excited about your book!

It appears unique in my experience!

Through the medium of well-selected readings and exercises, it exposes the student to a breadth of ideas comparable only to those found in the stacks of university libraries—which we know to be relatively inaccessible. It brings the "Mountain to Mohammed."

Simultaneously, its "grammar" section provides standards by which the serious student may establish for himself the quality of his work.

It is this self-discipline combined with the learning of established techniques that will enable the user of this book to be "at home" in any library—writing a scholarly paper, or simply learning for his own satisfaction.

CHARLES EDWARD DAVIS, Pastor,
San Mateo Presbyterian Church
San Mateo, Florida

Dorothy,

In thinking with you about the purpose and organization of the book you are now in the process of writing, *The Art of Communication: A Self-Help Course in Basics*, I am especially mindful of your long and varied career devoted to the development of the logical thinkng processes of the mind through the step-by-step analysis of one's own language.

If you will endeavor to leave for this generation of students, teachers and laymen what you have already given to that generation of students directly under your tutelage, the impact will be germane to that grain of corn first planted by the Pilgrim Fathers in New England, which has developed into the grain cultivated to feed the world.

The emphasis of this book on language study—its use and form—through grammar as an aid to logical thinking, which in turn helps in every phase of life, promotes a development of the mind and a conservation of the mental resources which civilization has provided mankind.

It is my sincere hope that those who read this book will find within its pages three things which you gave to me and my classes on Career Day at Jupiter High-Middle School in March of 1976 upon our first acquaintance: a hunger for knowledge and its assimilation for greater mental growth, a respect for the study of language forms as an aid to logical organization of thought, and a challenge to further explore man's linguistic past and development.

Mary Lou Warren
Teacher of English, Grade 8
Jupiter Middle School
Palm Beach County, Florida

Readers,

The Art of Communication: A Self-Help Course in Basics is a sequel to *America Is People and Ideas: Library Researching for the Space Age,* published by Exposition Press in 1966 for use in my freshman English classes at Palm Beach Junior College.

Self-help characteristics of this new book are supplied by writing assignments and the section on English mechanics, which had its beginning with junior high students and was refined in the junior college classroom. The 1966 text and classroom lectures produced what was characterized as "a refreshingly original approach to the study of any subject and one which opens many new doors to learning."

Now, in one unit, there are "conversations" to stimulate your thinking, together with basic rules of English mechanics to help you communicate your ideas. *The Art of Communication: A Self-Help Course in Basics* expects you to READ-THINK-WRITE, over and over, so that you can recognize your ability to proofread your own writing and thus see improvements in:

> your clarity of thinking,
> your vocabulary and understanding of words,
> your sentence structure (first for correctness, then for variety),
> your paragraph writing and your compositions,
> your production of a well-documented library research paper,
>   if you are college bound.

Easily distinguished division pages provide the dual purpose of supplying ideas to trigger your thinking, and sentences for grammatical analysis and study. Likewise, suggested assignments are easily found throughout the text. They may be followed in part, completely, or by being added to, according to your personal use of this text.

I hope *The Art of Communication: A Self-Help Course in Basics* retains the same overall interdisciplinary objectives of *America Is People and Ideas* which helps students relate today's space-age learning to the early pioneers through library researching and writing; encourages them to build concepts and ideas of their own for future learning experiences; represents, as one student phrased it, a "breakthrough to their thinking"; arouses scholarly excitement as students find themselves relating facts, ideas, and concepts within a discipline and, more importantly, among the disciplines.

The following comments of my colleagues and students illustrate what may become your own experiences:

"I have seen this course lead our students to realize that logical thought and clear expression are fundamental tools of living."

"Mrs. Peed, it seems to me, has accomplished what most teachers want to do: provide students with a key to a doorway that leads to greater learning."

"I have a whole new perspective in teaching my courses."

"I never realized how much knowledge can be acquired by going to the college library and working there."

"Relationships, combined with inquisitiveness, is the key to knowledge."

"The writing of a research paper is one of the biggest aids to maturing that will ever happen to you."

"The information began to pour from the books so quickly I felt like a child in a candy store."

"I am grateful to you for your efforts to improve the thoughts of a dull mind into a perceptive being who now believes learning is both enjoyable and fun."

ABOUT BASICS

Two words, seemingly unrelated, present themselves to my mind as I review the above comments and the expectations I have for this course. They are *Basics* and *Scratch*. Each is used colloquially today quite differently from the dictionary definition. In fact, the word *basics* as a noun, is not in any dictionary I have consulted. As used today, *basics* generally refers to the three R's, Reading, 'Riting, and 'Rithmetic.

Scratch is used today with pride to mean "created from basic elements," as when the cake at the local bake sale is marked "baked from scratch" to distinguish its construction from that of the cakes baked from a package mix. In its modern sense, then, *scratch* contributes to an understanding of the purpose of *The Art of Communication: A Self-Help Course in Basics* because it encourages you to analyze word elements, sentence parts, and paragraph construction—to begin from scratch, from the basics.

Carrying the comparison of *scratch* and *basics* one step further, and paralleling the definitions for scratch as a verb, noun, and adjective, we could say that what this course requires of you (as a verb) is *to work* at correcting your common grammatical errors in speech and writing, and *to learn* the accepted forms and rules of grammar; it requires (as a noun) *realizing* that the ability and ease in speaking, writing, and reading are the same as the capabilities of sport contestants who start from scratch—who receive no handicap; it requires (as an adjective) that returning to basics, by one's own efforts, is *acquiring the characteristics of*, and the self-assurance to be, one who starts from scratch because he is self-taught/self-trained, and has no handicaps. *He HAS the basics.*

The items that you will require to work through this self-help course are listed on the next page. Remember that *The Art of Communication: A Self-Help Course in Basics* anticipates that you will become more and more aware of your communicating ability as you increase in self-knowledge, self-confidence, and self-respect.

Be inventive. Watch your thinking and writing ability grow. But most of all enjoy your writing, even when it seems difficult.

DOROTHY MYERS PEED
Emeritus, Palm Beach Junior College
Hermits Cove, Satsuma, Florida

WORKING TOOLS

A GOOD DICTIONARY—one which will give you the derivation of words which are as important as the definitions when you build a vocabulary.

AN ENGLISH HANDBOOK—or access to one. This text does not purport to include more than a summary of English mechanics; it urges the use of a handbook for reference.

SCRAP PAPER—used paper with one side blank will do to write and rewrite sentences and paragraphs until you are satisfied.

LINED PAPER—for final drafts, which should be double-spaced for ease in correcting. These paragraphs should be numbered in their order of writing so that you can see progress in your work.

A FILING SYSTEM—or at least separate file folders, for work in grammar, the dictionary, paragraphs, library research, etc.

ACCESS TO A LIBRARY—or at least to a set of reference books for general information and research.

TWO KINDS OF NOTE CARDS—those like the samples on pages 212-13 for accurate reference book information; blank note cards in any size for notes on your readings.

A CRITIC/READER/CORRECTOR*—if you are fortunate enough to find one; or, if two students work together, each can indicate to the other how clearly ideas have been com-

---

*Suggestions for finding a CRITIC/READER/CORRECTOR: (1) Your local National Retired Teachers Association (NRTA); (2) your local American Association of Retired Persons (AARP), especially if there are secretaries or experienced writers in the group; (3) an in-service teacher tutor, if you are doing this work for College Level Examination Program (CLEP) credit; or (4) someone your local junior college recommends to you.

municated; or, best of all, you can be your own critic/corrector as you study and restudy the section on mechanics and apply the rules to your writing.

PATIENCE—as you weed out careless grammar errors in speech and writing.

PERSISTENCE—in finding the right word for your ideas as you capture them on paper.

PRIDE IN YOURSELF—in your newfound abilities, your patience and persistence and your accomplishments.

HOW TO USE THIS BOOK

CONSIDER your educational background, your age or working experiences, and your desire to communicate accurately, which is to say grammatically.

READ the "Procedure" for using the Thought Provokers and Sentence Structure Study, page 11.

STUDY the introduction to "Your Own Writings" on page 13. Note that the directions at the top of the page refer to the articles which follow in the section.

TURN to the "Note Well" information on page 136.

LEAF through pages 125 on to become acquainted with the grammar section, which will be referred to regularly.

DETERMINE to write, write, write. Only practice, patience, and persistence will make you a good communicator through writing, reading, speaking. Remember, clear thinking is basic.

ON EDUCATION

THOUGHT PROVOKERS
AND
SENTENCE STRUCTURE STUDY

The great end of education is to
discipline rather than to furnish
the mind; to train it to the use
of its own powers, rather than fill
it with the accumulations of others.

TRYON EDWARDS

*   *   *

PROCEDURE

The "Thought Provoker" pages which appear throughout this
book serve two purposes: to provoke thinking in preparation for
each writing experience, and to supply sentences to be analyzed
for their construction and punctuation.

Most of the quotations have come from *The New Dictionary of Thought* originally compiled by Tryon Edwards in
1877 and revised and enlarged by C. N. Catrevas and Jonathan
Edwards in 1955, published by Standard Book Company. They
will supply ideas to be enjoyed, to challenge your thinking, or
to initiate a conversation. Age and/or educational background
make no limitations; rather, they add to the variety of responses
that will be made.

Though there is a relationship between the quotations and the
substance of the pages which follow, there is no attempt to group
them by grammatical construction or punctuation. Reference to
the quotations as examples for Sentence Structure Study should

come about only when you believe you are ready for this study.

Your writings, which will improve as you work through the book, will include a variety of sentences which can be analyzed and corrected at the proper time. At first, be content just to transfer your thoughts to paper. Practice this without thought for structure or style for several exercises. Then, when you are writing your thoughts with a little more ease, write on every other line and begin to analyze and correct the sentences according to the information given in the grammar section. It is hoped that this section will be interesting reading as well as instructive. Then you will enjoy relating thought to structure because you NEED the rules of English mechanics to correct your sentence thoughts.

Note that ORDER is the thought of the quotations preceding the mechanics section. Occasionally, reference in this section to quotations as examples of rules will give you a start in discovering other examples of grammar and/or punctuation usage in the quotations. Don't hesitate to use your dictionary as a reference book. You will be surprised at the help you can get from the dictionary in basic grammar in addition to word study. Work! Enjoy!

YOUR OWN WRITINGS

READ this page.   WRITE the paragraphs.
STUDY the section following.   FILE. Later CORRECT.

These pages throughout the book will suggest writing exercises. At first you will write sentence thoughts, then thoughts which are paragraph length, and, finally, compositions. If you want to continue this study, a library researched paper will indicate your readiness for college and/or for CLEP credit.

Begin your file folder system now. Number consecutively your writing exercises so that you can observe your progress as you go along. Don't attempt to correct any of your exercises for a while, but follow the suggestions given on the previous page.

The final section in this book is a scholarly paper called a "colloquium" (Latin for *conversation*). It will supply examples of organization based on a lengthy group conference. It is written in a scholarly sentence and paragraph style with transitional words and ideas that give unity to the "composition." Be sure to study it well when you come to your final assignments.

* * *

In a sentence, state *why* you are using this book.

Read the following section and then write a sentence or two on *where*, if at all, you see yourself among the reactions listed in using grammar to aid mental health?

Why would a magazine article in 1961 and those referred to in 1976 have something in common?

Describe your first experience in using the card catalogue in the library. (See page 98)

Why do (do not) you agree with Emerson's definition of an American scholar in this interdisciplinary age? (See page 200)

A practical example of *recognized relationships of ideas* is important to your self-study: both a study of yourself and study *by* yourself. *Seeing* relationships of ideas is an important aid to intelligence. Discuss a time when you discovered seemingly unrelated ideas to have a relationship.

Write any other comments which come to mind in separate sentences. File these for future study.

13

USING GRAMMAR TO
AID BETTER MENTAL HEALTH

In September, 1960, I began teaching a basic English course in the Freshman Communications Department of Palm Beach Junior College. I soon found that the grammar techniques I had developed in the junior high level were readily applicable to more mature students and that when the combination of stimulating reading, thinking, and library researching was combined with the grammar study, the students actually *experienced* the difference between simple, compound, and complex sentences. They came to understand their *need* for different sentence constructions. At the end of the first semester, I contributed the following article to the *Junior College Journal* and was pleased to see it in print in the April, 1961, issue.*

Does the grammarian have an answer for the problem of pupil drop-outs in junior colleges? Educators in the early grades are concerned with teaching children how to live, how to understand themselves, and how to express themselves through the various media of self-expression. In this connection, the grammarian may have a vital point to make when he stresses the fact that a basic understanding of sentence structure is a fundamental concept which a pupil must understand and use with facility.

"The personality problem is large for drop-outs in school from the fifth to the twelfth-grade level," said Dr. Will Menninger in a program of the NET series entitled "Man's Search for the Meaning of His Life." The child who is confused may do wrong not so much from maliciousness as from ignorance. Ignorance of how to express his emotions, his thoughts, his individual ideas in such a way that he can be understood by those in his environment. If confusion is straightened out in his thinking, then he may also gain a set of values. In the process he may become acquainted with his thoughts, may know more about himself, and perhaps respect himself for having formulated his

---

*Used by permission of the American Association of Community and Junior Colleges, 1977.

own thoughts into spoken or written words which others may read and understand. Thus, as he communicates with others, he emerges with a feeling of self-respect and self-esteem which he has never before experienced.

How may the grammarian have a part in this self analysis? Simply by having a pupil analyze the subject and verb elements of his thoughts. First, the pupil must pinpoint the element of his confused thinking which concerns a topic idea. This he will label a subject. Next, he must recognize the action element of his thought, or the verb. Soon, the pupil's thought, clearly expressed, emerges.

Thus he has been encouraged to examine his thoughts, analyze them, and express them in understandable grammatical construction. He has, then, been stimulated to unlock his own thoughts, come to know himself better, and eventually realize that he has learned to think a little. With this systematic use of language, he may gain an appreciation for the linguistic system taught him in school. Confusion may dissolve before his ordered thinking, and gradually ignorance may give way to an understanding of self-expression which can be applied to all subjects in school.

That this expression is today delayed for so many years in a pupil's life is the present communication tragedy. The fact that it never develops for countless young people is even more tragic. It is wasteful to have basic English courses at the freshman college level so general in nature, when preventive teaching could have been done in the lower grades.

Palm Beach Junior College in Lake Worth, Florida, is proud of the work being done in a division of the Communications Department as a temporary stopgap which allows students who need basic English training to develop the tools which will spell increased personal understanding as well as more effective communication in future college written work. In this program the college is using a fundamental sentence structure textbook manuscript, soon to be published,* together with individual instructors' teaching techniques as the core material upon which to build a basic course in the understanding of grammatical sentence structure.

Several freshmen have recently written analyses of their accomplishments during a semester of this basic English program

---

*Emma Julia Phillips, *A Review of English Fundamentals*, (New York: Holt Rinehart and Winston, Inc., 1962).

which stresses sentence structure as the means of unlocking, stating, and developing thought accurately and easily.

> I find now that by learning to express my own idea instead of elaborating on other people's thought it has become easier for me to express myself. This is something that has always been a great problem with me. When I compare my paragraph writings at the beginning of the semester to the writings at the end of the semester, it just doesn't seem as if the same person has been writing them.
>
> To communicate, one must be exact in thought and knowledge of grammar, for it is grammar that gives us the accuracy and art to put across our thoughts as words. Still, it is through communication that this exacting science came about. This art is the science of man's communication.
>
> English has bored me through my high school years, but now it has taken on a new meaning. I remember when I wrote paragraphs that had no meaning, except perhaps to me. I have learned that the choice of a word may help express the point I am getting across. . . . I now realize my future hinges on whether I acquire a more understanding knowledge of communications.

From his first semester of basic English one student finds his writing ability greatly improved:

> Now I can just sit down and jot my facts down on paper, organize them, make an outline, and then start writing. In doing this I find myself writing my thoughts more quickly and easily. There has also been a boost in my grades.

Parents see results in improved sentence structure in the home in daily communication, and students find they read better. Two students summarize communication as an art and as a science in the following paragraphs:

> Few of us will ever be able to communicate with the world as some of our better-known poets and authors. Yet the science of communication can be mastered by any one of us who will give the time to study the grammar of our language. It is an honor to say what you have to say and be understood, and a privilege to speak words of beauty.
>
> The art of communication is something that most people take for granted all their lives. Speaking and writing are em-

phatic means by which we are able to express our thoughts, ideas, and beliefs. Without a complete understanding of this art, man is misinterpreted by others when he cannot convey his meaning and express himself clearly. With emphasis on advanced education and world progress today, people should realize the importance of communication in every phase of life, whether it is in the field of science or just everyday contacts with others. It is most important to be grammatically accurate in representing ourselves so that we shall not be misunderstood by others.

Watching students struggle with the frustrations of trying to express themselves when they do not have the basic concept of the subject-verb tools for expression is distressing. It is also wasted manpower. Students on the junior high level who are drilled in the use of these tools recognize them as vehicles for expressing thought, consider that they are being "furnished with a rock-bottom basis for studying languages," are grateful for being made to think through language and realize that it makes all school work more interesting, intelligible, and successful.

There are teen clubs to help children; young and old keep the body busy, exercised, and happy; then why not build English courses which will help exercise the mind, free it from some frustrations, and establish it as an honored and respected self? Teachers, too, will learn to look forward to the results such mental exercising can produce.

LEADING EDUCATORS VOICE CONCERN

The November-December, 1976, issue of *Today's Education* includes three articles which illustrate that the concerns indicated in the preceding April, 1961, *Junior College Journal* article have not changed much today. Many of the methods which brought forth outstanding results in the 1960s were devised to assure discipline and interest in the classroom. They were proven successful when "Get Peed, she'll teach you to think" was the advice given one student to another. Teaching challenges became more specific and individualized, then, as students learned that writing is not easy, that it requires practice, that it is self-satisfying and can be self-taught. Note that the professional field of each of the writers quoted below (see the footnotes) indicates how general is the present concern for improvement in the individual's thinking and communicating ability.

"Is There a Crisis in Writing Skills?" is the title of Richard Lloyd-Jones's article in *Today's Education*.* His summary statement is ". . . our Dis-ease about writing is probably chronic rather than acute." He explains that "hardly anyone is trained to teach writing, and often those who teach it write very little themselves." Then he adds, "Those who earn advanced degrees go out to a permanent job in which their status is determined by how quickly they get out of teaching writing." Lloyd-Jones quotes Bacon who said "Writing [maketh] an exact man," and adds "He [Bacon] was not worried about spelling, but he did take care with word choice and syntax and examples and quotations as they fit into his whole message. The point of the whole discourse depended on the exactness of the parts."

Lloyd-Jones believes that "writing can be taught. Teachers of composition can help students get information, select and arrange it, focus on what the arrangement means, and finally put it into words. These steps of discovery are at the heart of all education, and they are the key to good writing."

"A War on Fuzziness" by William Safire makes specific observations and suggestions. "As educators well know," he writes, "something is not working. . . . At home and at school, students have not been firmly directed to talk straight and write straight and think straight." He continues, "I'm not suggesting that we rap knuckles. I am suggesting that we set standards and make demands and begin at the root of communication: English. *Feeling* is easy; thinking is tough.†

To cure fuzziness, Safire says that "our schools should put a new emphasis on English . . . on straight talk and plain, clear

---

*Permission to print from *Today's Education* and Dr. Richard Lloyd-Jones who is Chair, Department of English, University of Iowa, Iowa City, and Associate Chair, Conference on College Composition and Communication.

†Permission to print from *Today's Education* and William Safire, who is a columnist for the *New York Times*.

writing." He thinks that "in our homes we ought to reinforce a new emphasis on the importance of language and wage war on fuzziness." He is sure that "career education fits into this accent on precision." He suggests that "just as the courts compel educators to let students have their say, so educators can demand that students demand their rights in clear, well-organized prose. It might provide them with new incentive to learn."

Finally, Madeline Hunter's article, "Right-Brained Kids in Left-Brained Schools," has helped me understand why, among other things, I designed a mechanical, nonverbal, method of teaching sentence structure and paragraph construction (see page 41 and 190).* She writes, "Now research has begun to sort the contents of that [people-are-different] basket into the categories of left- and right-brained thinking with promising and productive suggestions for teachers that could accelerate student learning in and out of the classroom.

"The left hemisphere has been called the temporal or propositional 'if-then' brain because it perceives significance and relationships across time. . . . The right hemisphere has been called the visual-spatial brain." She explains that "integrated brain thinking is the result of each hemisphere's augmenting information processes by the other." She points out, "Schools have been beaming most of their instruction through a left-brained input (reading and listening) and output (talking and writing) system, thereby handicapping all learners."

Madeline Hunter gives an example: "Students who can 'see' how a model airplane, for example, goes together use their more facile right brains and may not give their left brains the practice of reading and following directions for the model. Students who comfortably read and comprehend complex instructions use their left brains and may not give their right brains the practice of seeing how the parts go together."

It is evident from this research and my approach to teaching

---

*Permission to print from *Today's Education* and Madeline Hunter, who is principal of University Elementary School, Graduate School of Education, University of California, Los Angeles.

that I should be classified as a Right-Brained Teacher, for my
Kuder Preference Profile of long ago indicated my highest interests to be mechanical and scientific and my lowest to be
literary. Yet I have devoted a teaching career to helping students
relate the mechanics of English to their thinking and writing
processes. Phrased in the parlance of this article, efforts to inte-
grate both brains, in my own experience, have made me understanding and sympathetic with students struggling through what
is here called a left-brained school system.

A PRACTICAL EXAMPLE OF
RECOGNIZED RELATIONSHIPS OF IDEAS*

(Throughout this book you will be asked to relate ideas. This
section illustrates how relationships emerge from seemingly unrelated facts, events, or ideas. They may develop instantaneously
or over a long period of time.)

*What is the hardest task in the world? To think. I would put
myself in the attitude to look in the eye an abstract truth, and
I cannot. I blench and withdraw on this side and on that. . . . It
seems as if we needed only the stillness and composed attitude
of the library, to seize the thought. But we come in, and are as
far from it as at first. Then, in a moment, and unannounced, the
truth appears. A certain wandering light appears, and is the distinction, the principle we wanted. But the oracle comes because
we had previously laid seige to the shrine. . . .*

*We are all wise. The difference between persons is not in
wisdom but in art. . . . Perhaps, if we should meet Shakespeare,
we should not be conscious of any steep inferiority; no: but of a
great equality—only that he possessed a strange skill of using, of
classifying his facts, which we lacked.*

RALPH WALDO EMERSON

Today one does not have to be a Shakespeare or an Emerson
to develop an intellect. Mass media are so abundant and varied
in America that whoever wishes to think may develop his own
method of doing so. To quote Emerson: "What is addressed to

---

*Peed, *America Is People and Ideas*, pp. 179-86.

us for contemplation does not threaten us, but makes us intellectual beings. The growth of intellect is spontaneous in every step. The mind that grows could not predict the times, the means, the mode of that spontaneity."

As an example of this spontaneity and of classifying facts, I offer the example of astronaut Wally Shirra's space flight, especially that portion of his flight over the Indian Ocean.

For many years items of information had been collecting in my mind and notebook, until at the instant of a radio announcement at 11:33 A.M. on October 3, 1962, that the Sigma 7 Capsule had been sighted over the Indian Ocean, the full significance of the intertwining of many lives in the Draper and Maury families and the scientific significance of the life studies of these scientists struck me.

That the student may follow how one person's mind worked at that moment in history, the seemingly unrelated items are here listed and the student is invited to discover the interrelations and unique significances that may exist. In doing this the student may also draw upon his own background of information and quite possibly add other items to this somewhat personal sequence of thought-discoveries.

ITEM I. The *Miami Herald*, Wednesday, September 26, 1962.

Houston, Texas (AP).—*Schirra Mission To Include Light, Cosmic Ray Study.* Astronaut Walter M. Schirra, Jr. will be taking pictures of the earth, hunting rare types of cosmic rays, and checking on how much the earth's atmosphere reduces light during his scheduled six-orbit flight October 3. . . . The cosmic ray experiment will require no effort from Schirra. Scientists will attach packs of sensitive emulsions to each side of the flight couch. It is hoped certain rays about which little is known will strike the packs and leave impressions. . . . The experiment with light will be an effort to determine how much light filters through the earth's atmosphere and how well the astronaut can see at night.

ITEM II. The *Miami Herald*, Thursday, October 4, 1962.

Cape Canaveral (AP).—Here is a timetable on Astronaut Walter M. Schirra, Jr.'s historic orbital flight:
7:15 A.M. (EST)—Schirra was blasted off from Cape Canaveral atop a mighty Atlas rocket, the missile moving across the morning sky like a large, glowing star. . . .

10:23 A.M.—As Schirra zipped into his third orbit over Cape Canaveral, he shut off all controls and electrical power to allow the craft to move freely on its roll, pitch and yaws axes. Purpose of the drifting is to conserve control fuel and electric power. . . .

11:33 A.M.—Schirra was in contact with Muchea, Australia, and still in drifting flight. His suit temperature was still comfortable. *The Indian Ocean tracking station reported visual sight of the Sigma 7.* (Radio announcers commented at this point that the capsule compared in brilliance to the planet Venus.) Schirra said he still had 90 per cent of the altitude control fuel in his tanks. . . .

1:45 P.M.—Long drift period ends over South Africa, shift to automatic control. . . .

3:42 P.M.—Shifts to fly-by-wire control over Indian Ocean to assure proper attitude for firing of reverse rockets. . . .

ITEM III. A Western Union day letter, January 9, 1952.

Mr. Thayer Draper
Hastings-on-Hudson
New York

The staff of the Harvard College Observatory joins me in honoring the memory of Antonia Maury. Her life-long interest in astronomy and her brilliant contribution to the founding of the science of astrophysics will always be remembered in the history of man's knowledge of the stars.

HARLOW SHAPLEY
[Director, Harvard Observatory]

ITEM IV. *Time* magazine, March 21, 1949.*

SCIENCE
Whistle of the Missile

As rockets fly higher and higher toward empty space, it gets harder and harder to keep track of them. Telescopes have followed V-2's to about 100 miles up. But the slender WAC Corporal, which rose 250 miles above White Sands, New Mexico (Time, March 7), was too much for a telescope or

---

*Courtesy *Time*; copyrighted by Time Inc., 1949.

radar. What kept track of it was DOVAP (Doppler Velocity and Position), a new instrument designed for rocket-tracking by Army's Ballistic Research Laboratories at Aberdeen Proving Grounds, Maryland.

The Doppler Tells. Last week, Dr. Dorrit Hoffleit, 41, a dark haired spinster astronomer of the Harvard College Observatory, who helped develep DOVAP, explained how it works. A missile to be tracked by DOVAP carries a small radio transceiver (transmitter and receiver) which receives a radio wave from the ground, doubles its frequency, and relays it back to earth. But when the doubled wave is received on the ground, it is not exactly doubled. Because of the "Doppler effect," its frequency is changed slightly in proportion to the speed of the missile.† This variation, recorded as a sinuous line on a strip of movie film, measures how fast the missile is moving away from the receiving station. Four such records, from stations spotted about 14 miles apart around the rocket firing point, can be combined by a kind of triangulation to give the rocket's speed and position. Army Ordnance hopes that DOVAP will tell within six feet where the WAC Corporal was at every moment of its whole flight.

Silence at the Top. DOVAP's ground set has a loudspeaker which blares out the Doppler wave. As the rocket rises into the air and disappears from sight, the whistle of the missile tells listeners how it is doing. The sound gets shriller and shriller as the rocket gains speed. Then the pitch begins to fall as the rocket, its fuel exhausted, begins to slow down. The sound dies to a deep bass. Then comes silence as the rocket reaches the top of its flight. The sound starts again as the rocket begins falling. It rises to a piercing shriek and ends in sudden silence as the rocket hits the earth.

ITEM V. Notes From the *Dictionary of American Biographies.*

John William Draper

1811-1882

John William Draper was the son of John Christopher Draper, an English minister and amateur astronomer. He married Antonia Coetana de Paiva Pereira Gardner whose

---

†A body moving toward a receiver "crowds" the waves together, shortens them and thus increases their frequency. Moving away, it "pulls out" the waves, reducing their frequency.

family was attached to the court of Dom Pedro of Brazil and was descended from two sea captains, Paiva and Pereira, each of whom supplied and captained a vessel of Vasco da Gama's fleet which rounded the Cape of Good Hope and discovered the Indian Ocean.

Draper is best known for his work on radiant energy, the essential principle of the incandescent lamp. In 1857 he made the observation that "the occurrence of lines in the spectrum, whether light or dark, is connected with the nature of the substances producing the flame, and . . . if we're able to acquire knowledge respecting physical state of the sun other stars will be by examination of the light they emit." This was the first scientist in America to use diffraction grating. The grating was made for him in 1843 by the U.S. Mint.

He was also a pioneer in photography and took the first portrait of a person ever recorded by the sun. [The camera used in 1839 is now in Smithsonian Institution.] Draper sent a copy of this first picture to Sir John Herschel, the astronomer.

Henry Draper

1837-1882

Henry Draper was the son of John William Draper. He was an astronomer and pioneered in astronomical photography. He was reared in an atmosphere of culture and scientific thought. In 1860 Henry Draper built an observatory on his estate in Hastings-on-Hudson, constructed a grinding and polishing machine, and cast a 15½ inch mirror (speculum) as a reflector in his telescope. He added an ingeniously fitted mounting for photography with a plate holder driven, at first, by a sand clock. With this instrument a large number of photographs of the sun and moon were taken. With a later instrument Draper did his work in stellar spectroscopy and in May 1872 secured the first spectrum of a star, Vega.

ITEM VI. Personal letter from Antonia Maury to the Author.

Hastings-on-Hudson, N.Y.
October 25, 1951

Dear Dorothy,
I am glad to hear about this splendid conservation and garden club work you are doing for the schools. I can scarcely think of any more important subject for the coming generation to learn about than conservation of the soil and the need to preserve the balance of nature in all life.

Now it appears that the length of time that the generations of man will be able to live on this earth depends on the soil. The sun can continue to give light and heat enough for millions of years but the soil could be ruined in a hundred years or so, so badly that it could not produce food for us, and people and animals could not live. This could happen if we go on with the abuse we have given the soil in the past.

It is also a fine thing for grown people and children to have gardens of their own. Working in gardens in the sun is an excellent way to keep well and live long. And loving a garden, plants, and flowers is a great way of happiness.

It is a splendid thing that we are beginning to get all this into the schools.

With hopes for all success,

Yours,
Antonia Maury

❋   ❋   ❋

Let the reader now assume that it is 11:33 on the morning of October 3, 1962, and that the radio announcer has just reported the sighting of the Sigma 7 capsule with Wally Schirra aboard over the Indian Ocean. He can now understand why "Dorothy" of the letter in Item VI, now standing before a class of college freshmen English students, reached for the chalk, and wrote on the board: ANTONIA COETANA DE PAIVA PEREIRA* MAURY.

To quote Emerson: "What is addressed to us for contemplation does not threaten us, but makes us intellectual beings. The growth of intellect is spontaneous in every step. The mind that grows could not predict the times, the means, the mode of that spontaneity."

It was at that 11:33 moment in history that the association of the six items just listed was made in my mind and the realization came that this listing of seemingly unconnected facts and ideas would probably illustrate to a student what one process of thinking is: a process that is often long, seldom easy, but always rewarding.

It is to outline a process by which every student can share this most interesting and exhausting experience that this book has been written. It matters not on what level the student may be working when he uses this book; there are here researching,

---

*Paiva and Pereira are Portuguese ancestral names. Encyclopedia search will disclose seafaring relationships between these men and Vasco da Gama, the explorer who discovered the sea route around Africa to the Indian Ocean. (See the Genealogy Chart, page ?)

thinking, and writing tasks that can challenge a student many times over, and at many age or grade levels. Education is a continuous process, not bounded by IQs or ages.

In the college freshmen classroom situation just described, where students listened to radio reports on the Schirra flight for the first ten minutes of the class and then wrote their thoughts of the moment, the students generally found that the process of putting thoughts on paper was much simpler when the stimulus of interest and emotion dictated the words. Each reacted, of course, according to his own background of reading, interests, and general knowledge. The important point was that each was free to use his own mind and write whatever he was thinking. The results were therefore most interesting.

The late Mark Van Doren, Professor Emeritus of English, Columbia University, has characterized a student at such a time as a "happy student." He says, "The happiness of a student consists in his achieving to whatever extent is possible the freedom to use his mind. Nothing is more fun than using one's mind."

A practical result of becoming free to use one's mind is that one tends then to find the world intelligible and interesting in many, if not all, of its parts. And so, from October 3, 1962, at 11:33 in the morning to December 15, 1965, at 8:27 in the morning, the Space Age developed and a course in basic English was also put together. At the risk of being repetitive, I believe it significant to include the December occurrence here.

A LETTER TO WALTER SCHIRRA

December 15, 1965

To: Walter Schirra in Outer Space
From: Dorothy Myers Peed in Florida

At 8:37, a few minutes ago, you not only made outer-space history, but you also brought into complete circle an education project.

Here are the facts:

When you were up over the Indian Ocean in your first orbital flight, to be exact, at 11:33 A.M., the local radio station commented that your capsule had been sighted and that it appeared to be as bright as Venus.

My freshman English students here at Palm Beach Junior College were listening to this same broadcast on my transistor radio (preparatory, though they did not know it, to putting their thoughts down on paper when I turned the radio off). At the moment mentioned, ideas were suddenly related in my mind and I knew, without doubt, how I was going to unify material I had been encouraged to write up for publication. This sudden realization made me step to the chalk board, even as the broadcast was continuing, and write the following:

Antonia Coetana de Paiva Pereira Maury.

You see, for me, my "space age" began in 1924 when Antonia came to live in our home near the Tufts College hillside. In 1935, Harvard published her paper on the second binary star ever discovered, which she had studied following her uncle's and grandfather's astronomical work, work which had been turned over to the Harvard Observatory. I am referring to Henry Draper and John William Draper, respectively.

I was a young girl when Antonia came to live with us, curious and interested in everything she had to tell me about the lines in the spectrum which were "telling" her so many facts about these stars.

But it was more than spectrum analysis that she would talk about. She was an ardent student of Emerson; her granduncle was Matthew Fontaine Maury, the oceangropher; her sister was a famous paleontologist; her grandfather had taken the first daguerreotype of the moon from his home observatory in Hastings-on-Hudson, New York; and her uncle had developed the Draper Catalog of Stars. In addition she carried in her full name a reference to two Portuguese seamen who had been in Vasco da Gama's fleet when he discovered the Indian Ocean.

Now at 9:15 on December 15, 1965, I am standing before another group of Palm Beach Junior College freshmen who are taking their first college final exam. Again I turned the radio on in the last moments of your take-off, and so accustomed are our young people today to having sound in the background that they continued with their writings, stopping only for a moment on the take-off and first separation to indicate that they were doing two things at once.

But there is a good reason that they could do these two things at once.

Their examination consists of writing as much as possible of the body of their own research work, which has been done by following the Study Helps that are now a part of my book, which is, at this very moment, being printed to be ready for release in January, 1966.

The book refers to all that I have here described and is entitled, *America Is People and Ideas: Library Researching for the Space Age.*

This letter has been written on paper hastily borrowed from students and will accompany the autographed copy of my book, which I am proud to send you.

> Sincerely,
> Dorothy Myers Peed
> (Mrs. T. Brooks Peed)
> Instructor, Palm Beach Junior College

READINGS FOR THINKING AND WRITING

ON LANGUAGE

THOUGHT PROVOKERS
AND
SENTENCE STRUCTURE STUDY

There was speech in their dumbness language in their very gesture.

SHAKESPEARE

*Language is not only the vehicle of thought, it is
a great and efficient instrument in thinking.*

SIR H. DAY

Language most shows a man; speak that I may see thee; it springs
out of the most retired and inmost part of us.

BEN JONSON

*Language is a solemn thing: it grows out of life—
out of agonies and ecstasies, its wants and its
weariness. Every language is a temple in which
the soul of those who speak it is enshrined.*

D. W. HOLMES

There is no tracing the connection of ancient nations but by
language; therefore, I am always sorry when any language is
lost, for languages are the pedigree of nations.

SAMUEL JOHNSON

*Language is only the instrument of science, and
words are but the signs of ideas.*

SAMUEL JOHNSON

31

READ this page.   WRITE the paragraphs.
STUDY the section following.   FILE. Later CORRECT.

Write up a real or imaginary conversation or correspondence with some company because of an error (omission or what not) in the records kept by the computer.

Interesting library researching and writing on the computers and/or cybernetics could be done here. See the footnote of "Two Cultures" by Vannevar Bush for ideas.

Describe the characteristics and progress of speech in a child you have observed. Does this parallel the "NEED theory" developed in A Conversation about Language? How?

When the child goes through the *Why* stage, will this mean that he is using complex sentences? Explain.

*   *   *

After you have learned the "Eight Parts of Speech" jingle, on page 130, turn to your file of sentences and find some way to designate the parts of speech of as many words as you can. You will learn, later on, that many words can be used as several different parts of speech. Don't worry about that now; just see how many words you can identify using the jingle.

Based on your reading of "A Conversation About Language," go back over your sentences and make a diagram for each sentence (see page 41). Try to label each as Simple, Compound, or Complex. If you're having trouble, turn to page 41.

Now, take time out to study the section on Word Study including the Sidney J. Harris column on the value of a knowledge of Latin (page 129). This section is basic to both reading and writing.

Throughout this course turn to the Thought Provokers for writing experiences.

A CONVERSATION ABOUT COMPUTER LANGUAGE

(In 1967, Dale Washburn, Director of Data Processing at Palm Beach Junior College, and I taped a conversation about the relationship between the basic English I was teaching freshmen and his requirements for a successful computer programmer. In December, 1976, Washburn sent me the following message. He is the author of *Computer Programming—A Total Language Approach*, published by Holt in 1970.)

Dorothy,

I'm very glad to hear that you are writing a new book, *The Art of Communication: A Self-Help Course in Basics.* As you know, I'm convinced that there exists a real need for such a text. This is especially true for students in Computer Science, since they must learn to use a variety of languages in order to properly communicate with computers. One of their main difficulties arises when they fail to appreciate basic grammatical structure.

I know that you will remember our discussion, several years back, when I spoke of a computer language called COBOL (Common Business Oriented Language).

In COBOL the programmer communicates with the computer by using sentences, written in English, which form paragraphs. Such paragraphs are indented so that the computer recognizes the sentences as having an important break in the communication of commands. The sentences are constructed grammatically of verbs and nouns with a period used to indicate the completion of an idea. In fact, the computer realizes that it has not finished performing the function of the verb until a period is recognized. The verbs, as in ordinary use, denote action to be taken by the computer, and nouns are understood to be names where information is stored in the computer's memory.

Incidentally, if you misspell a word, the computer informs you that you made an error, because it's not sure what you are talking about. In such cases, you merely correct your spelling and resubmit the program to the computer for verification.

From this description, it should be apparent that in reality you are carrying on a conversation with the machine, a remarkable device which is quite insistent that you use proper grammar and demands that you tell it specifically what you want it to do. Any variation from the precise use of a particular verb will result in the computer's failure to perform your job.

Ironically, it now seems that I must teach grammar and proper use of the English language to be able to teach programming. So you see, there is a real need to get students back to the basics. If COBOL is not enough, we have a language called BASIC* which is a communication-oriented and conversational computer language—one which enables the student to carry on a conversation with the computer by means of a computer terminal. The terminals are video devices used to display messages being transmitted between student and computer. The advantage of using BASIC is that you can converse directly with the computer, in a truly conversational language. As you might guess, this particular language has become an important part of computerized education.

One very important feature of the latest computer development is the stress that is being placed on grammatical functions, especially syntax. Syntax is used by the computer to convey specific meaning. The computer will always follow a prescribed use for syntax even when the programmer thinks he means something else. And the computer is a real taskmaster when it comes to using the exact form of the verb. The computer assumes the programmer knows what he is asking it to do, and it applies the verb to the nouns in an exact order. Unfortunately, the programmer often is not that exact, and the results are not what he desired.

The basic problem that is encountered by a student in programming is determining from the results what was actually accomplished and whether, indeed, he has properly told the machine what he wanted it to accomplish.

---

*Look up basic English in your dictionary. Does the definition have significance here and not in the discussion on basics on page 6.

We find that students in Computer Science must become better students in English in order to communicate properly with the computer. Of course, they now see an important consequence of knowing the English language.

Ironically, a new problem has arisen. This occurs when a different programmer attempts to read and understand another's program. Since the language is prose, it often is not clear to another individual what the other person was attempting to do. In order to solve this dilemma, a new approach has evolved. This approach is known as structured programming, the basic function of which is to make programs written by other programmers more clearly understandable. To accomplish this, a set of rules has been developed to structure the basic elements of programming. The concept is quite analogous to the structure concepts employed in English. So you see, Dorothy, you are really working where "the action is." And as you can see, in this case, it is not the problem of man and machine-communication, but the problem between man and man-written communication. I truly believe that the world needs the type of book you are writing, and I quote, "The person who knows the grammar of his mother tongue can learn a foreign language easily." This is remarkably self-evident when that language is a computer language such as COBOL.

Dale W. Washburn
Director of Data Processing
Palm Beach Junior College
Lake Worth, Florida

A CONVERSATION ABOUT LANGUAGE

(I retired from teaching at Palm Beach Junior College in 1969. But my mind continued to ferret out ideas and devices to make more clear the relation between thinking and language. Freshman Communications was the title of the course I taught. The following is developed from classroom lectures on mankind's evolution of communications.)

Whether you speak impeccable English or are learning English as a foreign language; whether your speech is filled with idioms and slang, whether you speak a lingo or patois, you may find this conversation about language interesting. It is not designed to be an informative conversation, but a stimulant to your own concept of language and, it is hoped, to open up channels of thought that you have not as yet recognized.

Every conversation implies at least two conversants and is usually inspired by a remark, an observation, or a turn of events. It involves a speaker and listener, a writer and reader, as here, or a gesturer and observer; for language in any form is a transmission of ideas and emotions between living creatures by any means.

What precipitated this particular conversation? Three items from periodicals dated October, 1971. One is a syndicated columnist's article on Language Arts considering them the Key to Mastery of Any Field; a second is a staff reporter's newspaper report on a state Council of Teachers of English conference; and the third is the *National Geographic* magazine's article, "More Years with Mountain Gorillas," and, for our purpose here, may be considered research into the very beginning of language in its elemental sense.

To be specific, Sydney J. Harris concluded his column on the failure of young Americans to learn to converse in a foreign language with the statement, "Not one student in a thousand can conduct a mature conversation in a foreign language; they are too old, too busy and too indifferent to learn it." He believes that the "root of the trouble lies deeper than this; English itself is not understood by the mass of students. And when one does not understand the structure of one's own language, it is virtually impossible to learn a second, except by living abroad and hearing it every day."

He continues, "The whole body of language teaching—including English—in American schools needs a radical revision. And not merely for the sake of English (important as it is), but because ignorance in speaking and writing becomes a crippling handicap in all other subjects. If we cannot communicate coherently, we cannot achieve a mastery in any field. America is full of tongue-tied technicians who cannot transmit knowledge, even to their own countrymen."*

The newspaper report of a state Teachers of English Conference included a challenge to the teachers to stimulate as much student interest in grammar, vocabulary, and spelling as they do in English literature. "Bad grammar," the report said, "and construction do not necessarily make bad reporting, but I believe both contribute to a public loss of appreciation, respect for, and credibility in the media. Sloppiness in language leads to a loss of credibility and understanding, a weakness of the implicit authority of the printed word. And when print becomes sloppy and careless we have lost the precise communication between the reader and reporter."

The third article recorded a "conversation" between a gesturer and an observer which is an example of the basic definition of language as the transmission of emotions and ideas between any living creatures. *National Geographic* researcher, Dian Fossey's account of her three and a half years of study of the mountain gorilla reads in part:

> Two black hairy arms circled the tree trunk. A moment later a furry head appeared. Bright eyes peered at me through a lattice of ferns.
>
> I occupied a branch of another tree, slightly downhill from the gorilla who stared at me. We were both in a forest on Mount Visole in Rawanda, where I have been studying gorillas in the wild.
>
> The face was familiar, not only by its features but by its impish expression; it belonged to Peanuts, one of my favorite gorillas. He is a member of one of the groups I have studied closely, and that have grown used to my presence among them.
>
> Peanuts was wearing an expression I think of as "fun and games"; I have learned to recognize it in gorillas when they want to prolong a contact with me. Slowly, I left the tree and got down into the foliage to make feeding noises to reassure him.

---

*Sydney J. Harris. Column in the *Florida Times Union*, Jacksonville, Florida, October 21, 1971.

The moments that followed are among the most memorable of my life. They were particularly important to me because this was, in a sense, a farewell visit to the mountain slope. I was shortly to leave Africa for a prolonged stay in Cambridge, England, where I would begin working on a doctoral thesis and other technical reports of gorilla behavior.

Peanuts left his tree for a bit of strutting before he began his approach in my direction. He is a showman. He beat his chest; he threw leaves into the air; he swaggered and slapped the foliage around him, and then suddenly he was at my side. His expression indicated that he had entertained me—now it was my turn. He sat down to watch my "feeding" but didn't seem particularly impressed, so I changed activities; I scratched my scalp noisily to make a sound familiar to gorillas, who do a great deal of scratching.

Almost immediately Peanuts began to scratch. It was not clear who was aping whom. Then I lay back in the foliage to appear as harmless as possible, and slowly extended my hand. I held it palm up at first, as the palms of an ape and a human are more similar than the backs of the hand. When I felt that he recognized this "object," I slowly turned my hand over and let it rest on the foliage.

Peanuts seemed to ponder accepting my hand, a familiar, yet strange object extended to him. Finally he came a step closer and, extending his own hand gently touched his fingers to mine. To the best of my knowledge this is the first time a wild gorilla has ever come so close to "holding hands" with a human being. Peanuts sat down and looked at my hand a moment longer. He stood and gave vent to his excitement by a whirling chest beat, then went off to rejoin his group, nonchalantly feeding some eighty feet uphill. I expressed my own happy excitement by crying. This was the most wonderful going-away present I could have had.*

What an exciting and direct conversation! Neither anthropoid could possibly misunderstand the other. But the NEEDS in communication for the gorilla anthropoid in his group are so limited and minimal in relation to the NEEDS of Homo sapiens in her group that we can dismiss the gorilla's language at this point and begin the consideration of Homo sapiens's spoken language.

---

*Dian Fossey, "More Years With Mountain Gorillas," *National Geographic*, October, 1971, p. 574-77. © National Geographic Society, 1971. Used with permission.

Reports of the Tasadays, cave dwellers in a remote part of the Phillipines, make realistic a consideration of the cave man's intellectual development, which required a language and which illustrates the interrelation of language and intellect. Linguists have reconstructed the prehistoric parent language known as Indo-European. As a student, you may wish to pursue a self-directed library study of the scholars' understanding of this basic language. At the very least you will want to pursue a dictionary study of English words having an IE base, (see page 129).

Now let us bring semantics and syntax into our conversation and imaginatively enter upon a consideration of how man's language tools, their usage, and his intellectual growth may have been mutually related during man's prehistoric and historic development.

Let us think of early man as living in a cave community and of NEEDING to develop common terminology for things, for actions, and for ideas. (It is helpful in pursuing this approach to the study of grammar to consider the similar process a child goes through in learning to speak and build a vocabulary.) Our cave man first must attach particular sounds to individual things, and he must see to it that those around him respect and accept these sounds as names.

As an example we will consider the father and son relationship. The cave man must teach his son to hunt; hence, he must indicate various kinds of weapons such as rock, club, spear. Thus he has invented *nouns*, the naming words. The branch of linguistics called semantics has begun. Next he NEEDS to indicate various kinds of actions that the son must learn to perform, and he invents sounds like run, creep, throw, stab. He has invented *verbs*, the action words. But he also *NEEDS* to qualify the names (nouns) and the actions (verbs) in order to have these lessons in hunting be successful and productive. He NEEDS qualifying words: adjectives to describe nouns, and adverbs to modify the actions, the verbs.

Gradually he realizes that he can hold more than one idea in his mind at a time. He develops a NEED for joining words—for *conjunctions*. These new words hold together equal ideas; today we would call them *co-ordinate conjunctions*.

When he NEEDS to show the relationship of one noun to another, he prepares for this NEED by "positioning" a word, usually a short one, between the two substantives which are to be related. Expressed differently, he positions this new word in front of one of the nouns. Later, in the history of language, and especially English, this pre-positioned word which shows the relationship between nouns is called a *preposition*. It becomes so common and so useful that it is pre-fixed to the word. With the NEED for prepositions met, man's thinking has truly matured.

Homo sapiens's mind expands rapidly now, for the relationship between language and intelligence is a strong and productive one. Soon he puts nouns, prepositional phrases, and verbs together to express larger than word-size thoughts. A NEED for syntax, for sentence structure, has begun. Then he comes to the realization that the elements of thought to be joined together are not always equal, so he invents another kind of joining word—the *sub-ordinate conjunction*.

He is thinking in sentences and not just words, and his sentences are becoming more thoughtful all the time. He leaps from simple to compound sentences. When he recognizes relationships of ideas, he is ready to develop the *complex sentence*. But first he must have another kind of word which will allow him to relate a less important idea to the main idea in the sentence. He NEEDS *relative pronouns*. Finally, with subordinate conjunctions and relative pronouns, he can build all sorts of complicated relationships of thoughts and ideas. These are valuable and intelligent tools, for they make possible the *complex sentence*.

With the use of all these language tools for communicating and building mind power, mankind is developing even more valuable and intelligent relationships of ideas, facts, and concepts. He is reflecting intelligence and he is preparing for the ages through which he will pass.

Who can imagine an industrial, technological, or space age with only a simple or compound sentence to express thought!

The complex sentence is the important Key to Greater Learning.

The process of linguistic development, as suggested above, may now be summarized very quickly and mechanically. Here, the diagram for a substantive idea, or subject of a sentence, will be a dotted line, - - - - - ; that for the action and existence idea will be the predicate, ________ , a solid line.

A *simple sentence* would be diagramed as - - - - - ________ . One-word qualifiers (adjectives or adverbs) would not make a change in the pattern.

The combination of two simple sentences, or two independent clauses, would be represented by adding *and* to represent any coordinate, or pure conjunction. A *compound sentence*, then, would be - - - - ________ and - - - ________ .

With the need for prepositional phrases there would be an addition to these sentence patterns, but not a change in the basic pattern. If we use parentheses ( ) to represent the phrase, we could have a *simple* and *compound* sentence patterns as follows:

(1)   - - - -( )__( )__ Prepositional phrases in both subject

and predicate of a simple sentence.

(2)   ( )- - - - ________ and - - - - - - ___( )__ Compound sentence with the phrase in the first subject and second predicate.

It is man's progress in *thinking* that requires still another kind of sentence pattern. Thinking is based on relating ideas. In grammar this means relating the idea in a dependent clause to that in an independent clause. This describes a *complex sentence*. Since a clause contains a subject and a predicate, we will diagram it by using dotted and solid lines enclosed in parentheses (- - - ________). Clauses may be adjectival or adverbial; therefore, they may appear in either/both subject and predicates. Examples:

(1)   (- - - ________) - - - - _____________(- - - ________) Complex sentence; clause in subject and predicate.

(2) - - - - - - ( ) - (--- ______) Complex sentence;
phrase in subject, clause in predicate.

(3) - - - - - - - - - - ______( ) and - - - - ______(--- ______)
phrase in predicate (conjunction) clause in predicate.
Compound-complex sentence—Why?

This conversation about language has summarized the facts you may already know about the mechanics of English. I hope it has suggested other ideas for you to consider in the evolution of language from prehistoric times. If formal grammar has bored you in the past, perhaps now there is a new significance in what may have been man's first scientific invention—oral communication between intelligent beings.

ON FATE AND INTUITION

THOUGHT PROVOKERS
AND
SENTENCE STRUCTURE STUDY

You conquer fate by thought.

THOREAU, *Journal*, May 6, 1858

There is no energy shortage. There is no energy
crisis. There is a crisis of ignorance.

R. BUCKMINSTER FULLER

I'm absolutely convinced that the only kind of planning has to be
for world man. . . . Each place around the world has its uniqueness, and the uniqueness here in Maine is in the great tides and
the fogs and the lovely wilderness which is still here.

R. BUCKMINISTER FULLER

in a TV interview in 1968

Again and again,
Step by step,
Intuition opens the doors . . .
Toward the physical and metaphysical success
Of all humanity.
And because its design
Permits humanity to live anywhere
Around our planet's watery mantle
And because this sailing craft
We are now to launch
Is the epitome of design competence . . .
We herewith give
To this world-around dwellable
High-seas sailing craft
The name—INTUITION.

R. BUCKMINSTER FULLER,
from the cover of *his* book *Intuition**

---

*By permission of R. Buckminster Fuller.

READ this page.
STUDY the section following.

WRITE the paragraphs.
FILE. Later CORRECT.

For the first time in your writing exercises, think of a paragraph-size idea which requires several sentence ideas to go beside (para) one another to complete the thought. See "The Thinking Chart" page 126 for a comparison of sentence-size and paragraph-size thoughts.

The following material on R. Buckminster Fuller will give you many opportunities to select topic ideas for paragraphs. You should write several paragraphs from this section. But don't be concerned, this time, about what or where your topic sentence is, or *if* you have a topic sentence in the group of sentences you are calling a paragraph. Just try to have all the sentences have some relation to the main thought in the paragraph.

*   *   *

HERE ARE SOME IDEAS FOR WRITING PARAGRAPHS. ADD OTHERS OF YOUR OWN.

Is "synergy" in your dictionary? What about "livingry" and "weaponry"? Look up -ery and -ry to see what the dictionary says about these suffixes on words. Did Bucky, as his biographer calls him, manufacture words for the purpose of illustrating his points? Did this help in his "favorite way of describing the state of the civilized world"?

React to Bucky's idea that chemistry was a more important subject for an architect to study than advanced mathematics. Include a discussion of synergy, if you wish.

If you had been an architectural student listening to one of Bucky's lectures, what would have been one message he would surely have brought to you? Explain the message and the fancy name he had for it.

*   *   *

At this point in your work, begin reading "with a pencil," which means to underline ideas that interest you, and/or make notes in the margins to reflect your thinking as you read: *You can learn to write by reading.*

WIZARD OF THE DOME*

From Afghanistan to Montreal, from St. Louis to Honolulu, people have seen geodesic domes in spectacular use. But the American genius who created them has become almost a legendary figure instead of a real man living and working today. Here is the inventor himself, a man with the courage of his convictions, who faced a hostile society on his own terms, and won.

Buckminster Fuller's special "geometry of nature" had led him to other products before the dome, such as his Dymaxion houses and cars. It is leading him to others— a design that is more concerned with people than mechanics. All are described in this book by an author who knows the man and understands the principles of his inventions. Sidney Rosen has told a dramatic, modern success story.

> From the book jacket, Wizard of the Dome:
> R. Buckminster Fuller,
> Designer for the Future
> by Sidney Rosen

His years in the Navy were a time of intense learning for Bucky. He spent much of his spare time reading books on architecture, engineering, mathematics, aviation, industrial design, and philosophy. His brain sucked ideas up out of these books like a vacuum cleaner. And in his mind, he began to sort out those ideas which seemed especially important for man's struggle against the forces of nature. He tried to figure out the directions in which civilizations were moving. At the moment, he was unable to work out anything that made sense. Later in his life, the pattern became clearer. . . .

What Bucky wanted was the lightest possible material that could support the greatest possible weight. The success of his ideas would be based upon using *the least to accomplish the most*. Bucky found the one word that expressed what he expected technological research to do for the housing industry.

**Sidney Rosen, Wizard of the Dome: R. Buckminster Fuller, Designer for the Future (Boston: Little Brown and Company, 1970). Reprinted with permission.*

*That word was *synergy.*

†Synergy was a word that you might not find in everyday conversation, but it was a word well-known to chemists. It meant the behavior of a whole system that could not be predicted by the behavior of any of its individual parts. For example, chemists knew that there were two chemical elements, sodium and chlorine, that differed not only in their appearance, but also in their individual behavior. Sodium was a soft, silvery metal that burst into flame the moment it touched water. It certainly could not be eaten without burning and poisoning the eater. Chlorine, on the other hand, was a heavy, greenish gas, also very poisonous to man. But if these two elements were allowed to come together and react, the result was a white-appearing crystalline substance called sodium chloride. And this stuff was far from poisonous; it sat on the tables of most American families in saltshakers! Thus, the whole system called sodium chloride had neither the appearance nor properties of its two individual components.

‡Bucky saw that man had to begin thinking in terms of synergy; that is, if man wanted to use science and technology to the best advantage. It was not the individual parts of nature that were necessarily most important; it was the *integrated behaviors* of these parts. He realized that there were many blessings of synergy waiting to be discovered: new metal alloys which could lead to the manufacture of new machines and engines; new ways of using radio waves and radio circuits. Why couldn't light energy be changed into electrical energy that could be used to open doors or control machinery?

There was plenty of useful energy in the universe, energy that existed in many different forms. When you rubbed your hand against a table, your hand became warm; that was mechanical energy being changed into heat energy. Growing plants were always changing the sun's radiant energy into the chemical energy of growth. In radio stations, sound energy was being changed first into electrical energy and then into electromagnetic energy. Radios that caught that electromagnetic energy in their antennas simply reversed the energy transformation.

---

*Transitional idea. (See Paragraph Patterns on page 190)
†Patterns II and III.
‡Pattern V.

The more Bucky thought about changing light energy into electrical energy that could be made to do mechanical work, the better the idea seemed. Was it possible? He dashed off a letter to his brother, Wolcott, who was working as an engineer for the General Electrical Company. Did they manufacture any kind of radio tube that was sensitive to light? Could such a tube be hooked up to an electromagnetic relay that would activate switches?

Wolcott's return letter was devastating. There was no such tube. And with great humor, Wolcott had concluded his letter with, "Bucky, I love you dearly. But can't you make it easier for your relatives and friends by not including preposterous ideas?"

Bucky received somewhat the same reception when he went to a company that manufactured aluminum metal for industry. He questioned the engineers about the possibility of a strong aluminum alloy that could be used as a framework for houses. He wanted to use such an alloy in his dirigible house.

But the engineers shook their heads. Strong aluminum alloys to be used in house-building? It was a preposterous idea! Aluminum was good for making coffeepots and souvenirs. It was a soft metal, and would always be used only where soft metals were useful. When Bucky began to talk to them about synergy and the chances of finding his alloys, the engineers became coldly polite and said good-bye.

*Bucky was undismayed by such failures.

†He kept planning his dirigible house. The decks would be held in place by tension cables, yet the whole house would be light enough to be lifted up and moved by a zeppelin. After all, the rapid progress of aviation was bound to change man from a stationary, root-putting-down condition to a mobile, "to-ing and fro-ing" state. If the airplane was shrinking the earth in size year by year, then a man should not have to be bound to a specific stationary dwelling in a specific place.

‡What man needed was a home that could be transported by air and put down anywhere on earth, at the North Pole or in the Sahara Desert. Such a house would have to be self-sufficient, carrying its own power, water (which would be

---

*Transitional idea.

†Pattern I.

‡Pattern IV.

reusable), and disposal units. Bucky thought of the earth as the "Air Ocean World," where air travel could make it possible for man to locate himself in places that had always been considered inaccessible. Synergetic discoveries would provide ways for man to control hostile environments that were too cold, too hot, or too stormy. It was time to begin thinking of a universal shelter that could be used by anyone anywhere. . . .

Bucky eventually designed a shelter. But what to name it! Finally, an advertising man to whom he talked had the idea that Bucky should talk to him about his "house" and, as he did so, he would write down what he thought were Bucky's key words.

> Bucky began to talk, while the advertising man scribbled notes. Finally, he interrupted Bucky in the middle of a sentence.
> "Look here, Mr. Fuller, your talk is full of scientific terms. But I notice that there are some words that turn up over and over. Here are three of them: *dynamic, maximum, ion.* I know what the first two mean, but what's an ion?"
> "That's an atom that has gained or lost electrons and has become an electrically charged particle."
> "Hmm, ion—well, that's scientific enough. What if I put together the first syllables of dynamic and maximum, and then add ion. Dy-max-ion—by golly, that's it!" He pounded a fist into his other hand in excitement. "There's the name for your modern house—the Dymaxion House!"
> Bucky's eyes gleamed behind his thick glasses. He tasted the word on his tongue. It had a fine futuristic sound. *Dymaxion.* He shook his head vigorously up and down, saying yes. It was a perfect name.
> The pleased advertising specialist shook Bucky's hand. "It's your word, Mr. Fuller. I'll see that Marshall Field and Company patents it in your name."
> A warm glow spread through Bucky's body. Finding the new name was a good omen. He did not yet know that all his future work would be stamped with the Buckminster Fuller trademark—DYMAXION. . . .

Finally, Bucky, through his practical knowledge and development of his own relationships of ideas, together with his determination to create better housing concepts, arrived at the geodesic dome.

By 1959, more than a hundred companies had been licensed to manufacture geodesic domes. Some of these were "plydomes," made of bent pieces of plywood and used as playhouses in parks and playgrounds. Others were huge affairs, costing as much as two hundred thousand dollars each. The Union Tank Car Company built and installed such a dome, three hundred and eighty-four feet across, at Baton Rouge, Louisiana. This dome, which could accommodate an entire football field and stadium, was large enough for whole trainlengths of railroad cars that needed rebuilding. A similar dome was built at Woods River, Illinois. There was a geodesic dome over the Anheuser-Busch Park aviary in Tampa, Florida, and another over that dolphin playground, the Seaquarium, at Miami. In a Cape Cod restaurant, delicious seafood was served up under one of Bucky's domes. And in St. Louis, Missouri, a paradise of tropical foliage and flowers began to flourish in a temperature and humidity controlled atmosphere under a great aluminum and plastic dome called the *Climatron*. In addition to designing and consulting fees, Bucky's corporations received five percent of the sales price of every dome made by a licensed manufacturer.

Airline stewardesses all over the world began to recognize the chunky man with the thick glasses who seemed to be going from one country to another throughout the year. No matter how long the flight, his temper was always even and his smile pleasant. He traveled several thousand miles in a jet as calmly as other men might drive down to the corner drugstore.

The message that Bucky brought to the universities he visited and to the students whom he addressed was always about the part they would play in the future of man's existence on earth. He warned against overspecialization—that was the path to doom for mankind. Look at the different biological species that had disappeared from the face of the earth. Look at the human tribes that had become extinct. They had grown overspecialized, each in its own way—and could not adapt to sudden change.

This was precisely what Bucky's business was—being ready for change before it came. His name for this activity was *comprehensive anticipatory design science*. But politicians and industrialists had no interest in this kind of science. They cared little about the *ecology* of man, that is, about the balance between man and his natural surroundings. Look at the atmospheric pollution in the cities. Witness the wholesale destruction of forests and the indiscriminate use of insecticides. These were the results of specialization. Corporations were interested in specialization, because specialization provided them with a means of making money. Over and over, Bucky told his audiences:

"No scientist has ever been retained, or hired professionally, to consider the scientific design of the home of man, to consider objectively the ecological pattern of man, to design ways of employing the highest scientific potential towards helping man to be a success on earth, to implement total man to enjoy total earth. No scientist has ever been retained to do such a task. And we speak of our age as the *age of science!*" . . .

Most older architects still found it difficult to accept Bucky. When asked, they would often reply that it was true Bucky was a man of genius, a great inventor, a fine engineer, "but he's not an architect, you know!"

*On the other hand, Bucky was not afraid to tell young students of architecture what he thought was wrong with the profession. The architect, he pointed out, had sold himself down the river to the people who were making fortunes developing real estate. These operators hired architects, told them what kinds of houses to design, what materials were to be used, and where the materials would be purchased. The architect really designed nothing and originated nothing. He was just a slave to the real estate business.

†What a young architect needed to know, Bucky said to his audience, was more than drawing, more than architecture. He had to go into airplane factories and learn about production engineering and tools and metal alloys. An architect without an understanding of the most advanced technology was a useless architect. For example, Bucky felt that chemistry was far more important to the architect than advanced mathematics; yet at most schools of architecture students often had little or no chemistry and three or four years of the calculus. But in chemistry was where you learned the rules by which nature structured materials, the materials that architects would be using in their work.

---

*Pattern II.
†Pattern III.

Architects, argued Bucky, had to become the opposite of specialists. The specialist took things apart; the architect put things together. He was a *comprehensive* person. It was up to the architect to help keep the world from falling apart. But before he could do that, the teaching of architecture in the schools would have to change. Architecture would have to be taught as an important part of comprehensive anticipatory design science.

Bucky had a favorite way of describing the state of the civilized world. There were two major divisions of man's activity: *weaponry* and *livingry*. Major scientific advances had always been made in the name of weaponry. Thus, the armies of the world were equipped with costly electronic equipment for warning, destroying, and killing. But in the cities of the world, millions of people were still living in horrible slums. The peaceful arts that were concerned with improving man's shelter and well-being were low-priority arts, compared with the high priority of weaponry. So livingry was an underdeveloped area. Progress in livingry was made only in a kind of accidental way, as a by-product of the rapid technical advances made by weaponry. Perhaps this was one reason that engineers and scientists had lost communication with the people in literature and the fine arts.

"If you gain the lead in the world's design science," Bucky would tell his young audience, "and apply it to *livingry*, then there is hope. But you don't have much time. The weaponry industry is ready to invade the livingry field. If that happens, a dreadful fate awaits humanity. Man will become totally godless, and his life will be governed by decisions turned out by a computer. You the teachers, and you the students, are man's hope."

ON LISTENING

THOUGHT PROVOKERS
AND
SENTENCE STRUCTURE STUDY

To listen well is as powerful a means of influence as to talk well, and is as essential to all conversation.

A single conversation across the table with a wise man is worth a month's study of books.

Chinese Proverbs

It is good to rub and polish our brain against that of others.

Montaigne

Conversation is an art in which a man has all mankind for competitors.

Emerson

Conversation is the laboratory and workshop of the student.

Emerson

Conversation opens our views, and gives our faculties a more vigorous play; it puts us upon turning our notions on every side, and holds them up to a light that discovers latent flaws which would probably have lain concealed in the gloom of unagitated abstraction.

Melmoth

53

READ this page.   WRITE the paragraphs.
STUDY the section following.   FILE.. Later CORRECT.

To suggest writing subjects based on the next section is useless. The only valid ones are those which will come from your own experiences—remembrances of conversations, events, or special convictions which the conversations suggest. Use the bottom of this page to write your own topics as they come to your mind or are based on your underlinings or marginal notes. This practice will associate your thinking with your reading and will, in turn, be reflected in your writing.

After you have written several paragraphs on your notes or the quotations on any of the preceding divisional pages, it would be well to turn to the section on English mechanics (page 125).

Read these pages carefully. Some readers may need to spend considerable time studying the rules and examples. All will want to use the quotations for Sentence Structure Study based on these pages of study. Exclude the pages on paragraph writing for now, and turn to all the papers you have in your file folders. If you already have some paragraphs written on every other line for easy correcting, begin with these and see how much you can improve your sentence structure, word usage, punctuation, and any other basic material you have studied. Use your dictionary to check your spelling.

Study pages 171 to 176 on punctuation.

*   *   *

Now study the Thought Provokers throughout the book for examples of the punctuation discussed.

LIST BELOW WRITING IDEAS FOR THIS SECTION:

LIST BELOW THE ENGLISH MECHANICS YOU MUST STUDY FURTHER:

RECOLLECTIONS OF KITCHEN TABLE
CONVERSATION

In 1924, Antonia Coetana de Paiva Pereira Maury came to live in our home on Tufts University hillside, away from the often fogbound Charles River area of the Harvard Observatory. Miss Maury was an ASTRONOMER and had just discovered that the star she was studying, the Beta star in the constellation Lyra, was a double star—the second double star then known. She had had a part in the Harvard study of the first binary, and now she had decided to apply the Draper idea of studying a star by photographic spectrum analysis to "her" binary star study. This would be a lengthy study, she believed, and so she wanted to live on the hillside where, she hoped, the air would be clearer than along the river. On this thin thread, then, began my association with CONSERVATIONIST, ORNITHOLOGIST and ASTROPHYSIST Antonia Maury.

She prepared her own meals in our kitchen at the strange hours of 11:00 A.M. and 11:00 P.M. Often I sat with her and was fed, not with food, but with conversations which certainly were ready-made for a high school student who would enter on a liberal arts course at Tufts, and, eventually, become a teacher.

Many times I went to bed with my mind in great confusion. What, I tried to understand, do lines on a spectrum have to do with learning how far apart the twin stars she was studying were? how far were they from the earth? how fast were they rotating around each other? of what were the stars composed? My Space Age had already begun, though I did not know it. Certainly I did not have newspaper articles like that on page 89 to describe how Antonia's uncle, Henry Draper, "had revolutionized theories of solar spectrum." Nor had I then seen the pencil-size hole in the outer wall of her grandfather John William Draper's home in Hastings-on-Hudson whereby he studied a SPECTRUM

____

Note: Capitalized words refer to topics beginning on page 201.

of light and the spectra caused by the burning of many different substances.

I could understand, however, that, because of the importance of these studies by her grandfather and uncle, she would want to carry on their work through the study of "her binary" by the spectrum analysis method. It was important that the work be done at Harvard Observatory (now a part of the Smithsonian Institution) where the telescope used by the Drapers had been given in their memory. Harvard published the results of her many years of study in 1935, and it was immediately considered basic in astrophysics. Dr. Shapley's telegram at the time of her death to Thayer Draper, Antonia Maury's nephew, notes "her brilliant contribution to the founding of the science of astrophysics," saying that "it will always be remembered in the history of man's knowledge of the stars." See page 22.

"Grandfather said," would preface many of Antonia's comments to me at the kitchen table, usually late at night. When she would put her elbows on the table and entwine her fingers, while a special reminiscent expression would come to her eyes, I knew I would be hearing about John William Draper, PHILOSO-PHER and HISTORIAN. As a philosopher he wrote *History of the Conflict Between Religion and Science;* as a historian he wrote *History of the Intellectual Development of Europe.* His three-volume *History of the American Civil War* was based on the United States Secretary of State's records and his own concept of geography and of the effect of climate on immigration and politics, thus seeing the causes from a unique point of view.

Sometimes, "Emerson said," would reflect the course she took with the Concord blacksmith who had served and appreciated Emerson. A box of notes and research awaited her leisure to write her own comments on Emerson.

There were many other Draper accomplishments for me to pass on to students for their own research and study. For instance, Dr. Draper, CHEMIST and PHYSICIAN had studied capillary attraction in blood cells, a project which was later the basis for the study of blood in relation to the amount of carbon dioxide present. Students of nursing in my classes regularly found

Draper's name in their readings and were often inspired to do research of their own on the characteristics of blood. Draper was the first chemistry professor at New York University and became president in 1850. He is credited with considerable responsibility in establishing New York City as a medical center.

Antonia's accounts of her grandfather's work with Samuel F. B. Morse always interested me. Her grandfather, she said, helped Morse lay out miles of wire in a field near the college so that Morse could prove his invention of the telegraph. Morse and Draper were colleagues on the faculty of New York University. Morse was head of the Art Department, and Draper was head of the Chemistry Department, a combination which student researchers discovered had great significance in the development of photography.

Morse went to France to see artist Louis Daguerre and found him attempting to use sunlight in the picture-making process which had already been named for him, the daguerreotype, but he was not completely successful. Morse returned to the States with the incomplete process and proposed that his chemist friend work on it. He did. In 1839 the first picture of a human face made in full sunlight was taken of Draper's sister, Dorothy. She sat with white powder on her face on the roof of a university building and Draper focused his camera through a vat of sulphuric acid, taking ten minutes for the exposure.

DRAPER, the SCIENTIST, was interested in what this accomplishment meant to the astronomer and sent the original photograph to Sir John Herschel in England. The Draper camera finally went to the Smithsonian Institution. A copy of Aunt Dorothy's picture was always on Antonia's bureau, but our family was not fully aware of the significance of the picture.

As described in the newspaper article on page 89 on moon photography, the Drapers, father and son, went on to use the camera in their astronomical research while another son put the camera to the eye piece of a telescope and so was the first to illustrate a medical paper with photographs instead of drawings.

In 1962, a STUDENT who made a study of the history of

photography wrote: "From a drop of mercury on a silver plate to the ten-second countdown of astronaut John Glenn, a man is building a web of life from a network of relationships."

Antonia Maury was a charter member of the Massachusetts Audubon Society. As an ORNITHOLOGIST she would show her concern for birds in the winter by scattering grain on the snow as she walked from home to transportation to the observatory, and she always had a container of suet outside her window for winter feeding. As a CONSERVATIONIST she was one of the pioneers who kept their eye on Washington to follow legislation affecting conservation of wild life and of water, the preservation of certain trees, and of an island where the brown bear bred. Pollution and smog were not common terms in her day, but she would have been the first to understand the significance of the problems.

From the beginning of my teaching I tried to make students aware of "the good earth" and of "man's responsibility as its keeper." In 1951 I asked Antonia to write something about conservation for me to use in the Junior Gardeners' display in the Community Garden Show. She wrote me the letter on page 24 which I used as a memorial to her, for she passed on three months after she wrote the letter, and just before the garden show. The letter and display took the highest honors, but one sentence went on to stimulate many junior college students to do research on every possible phase of conservation. She wrote in October 1951:

> The sun can continue to give light and heat enough for millions of years, but the soil could be ruined in a hundred years or so, so badly that it could not produce food for us, and people and animals could not live.

They would compare the "hundred years" that Miss Maury had given them with the number of years already passed since 1951, when they were writing, and be not a little concerned for the future. She would have approved of developing solar energy.

Then Came the Space Age Sputnik—1957

As if the Draper-family accomplishments were not enough for Antonia Maury to inherit, the Maury genealogy now became significant as we moved into the Space Age and added ocean space to outer space in our awareness. For me there were also new recollections.

In 1957 when Sputnik went up, I was teaching on the junior high level and pondering how to teach grammar so that it would have significance throughout a student's life as a tool to help clarify his thinking, speaking, reading, and writing. One girl had begun the answer to my question on the first day of school after Sputnik went up, "How will Sputnik affect the education of those of you now in junior high?" with the statement, "One nation has this day put its hand through the unknown."

Students were evidently ready to think, and I had an abundance of up-to-the-minute subjects to trigger their thinking if I included the many references Antonia had made to Matthew Fontaine Maury, her grandfather's cousin and the Father of Oceanography. Here was a name now looming as large on my Space Age screen as those of the astronomers and their accomplishments. Surely the Gulf Stream, whales, Cyrus Field and the Atlantic cable were ocean space subjects to be reckoned with.

So, I developed a group library project, with the assistance of the librarian, and took a class at a time to the library, each with an individual subject that was related in some way to Antonia Maury. The students read, took notes, prepared oral reports to give to their classmates, and, finally, developed a paper which they called "This Is Your Life, Antonia Maury." They were proud of their accomplishments and suddenly knew what I meant when I said to them in the classroom, "Give me eye attention."

Eye Attention

The kitchen table conversations that I had with Antonia Maury taught me more about one's thinking processes than I realized. A Tufts course in the development of thinking, given by a professor whose eyes reflected his enthusiasm for his subject, made me recognize this enthusiasm in Miss Maury's eyes. I both saw and *heard* her thoughts develop. As my mind strained to take in her remarks, I am sure my eyes reflected confusion, for she often repeated explanations of her scientific work for me without my asking. These observations led me to require "eye attention" in the classroom whenever I wanted to be sure the students' thoughts were following the presentation. The students and I came to realize that the custom of relating thoughts with physical expressions, as of the eyes, assisted them in developing their thoughts into written and oral form. They learned to recognize that confused thinking produced confused sentences and came to the conclusion that, often, both the thought and the mechanics of the sentence must be worked on to develop an accurate and correct sentence. Eye attention, therefore, meant: RESPECT YOURSELF AND YOUR ABILITY TO THINK. YOU CAN LEARN TO PUT YOUR THOUGHTS ON PAPER.

In 1960, when I began teaching at Palm Beach Junior College, I used all these techniques in a library researching and writing unit with such success that it became the outline of the entire course. The material was certainly ungraded and not limited to any age level, and a grammar review was always timely. Students often developed a career interest through this individual reading-writing medium, for, as an interdisciplinary course, practically any subject was permissible to pursue.

INTIMATE VIRGINIANA: A CENTURY OF MAURY TRAVEL BY LAND AND SEA

One more kitchen table "legend" was recalled when I met Anne Fontaine Maury Hirschfeld and she told me of her book, *Intimate Virginiana: A Century of Maury Travel by Land and Sea.* She said she had opened a trunk in her father's attic to find it full of Maury family letters carefully preserved by Aunt Ann, the consul James Maury's only daughter, and she had published these letters in 1941. I could use any I wanted in my class work and/or in the text I was developing, she said. She had based her book on "The Old Consul, James Maury," as the grand old man of the family. Suddenly, I realized that this must be the same James Maury who was Antonia's great-grandfather—another legend became reality. One evening Antonia had recounted her conversation at the passport office in Boston where she had just obtained a passport to travel in Europe. To their question of her citizenship she had answered, "My great-grandfather was appointed by George Washington to be our first consul in Liverpool, England." Now, in a moment, the Maury name became as alive as the Draper name, and here, in addition, I had an entire book of people, occupations, accomplishments to add to the student lists already brimming with interest.

Through Mrs. Hirschfeld there was another, more intimate tie, too. She had known Dr. Carlotta Jauquina Maury, Antonia's paleontologist sister as well as I had known the astronomer; neither of us had met the other sister, so we had much to talk about.

I completed *America Is People and Ideas: Library Researching for the Space Age*, my first book, quickly, now, with this gift of Maury family letters. When it was published in 1966 I worked out a Maury-Draper Genealogy Chart which interested students of U.S. History and built social awareness and pride of country in many readers' minds. Even an interesting neighborhood romance became evident when records showed that Virginia Draper had grown up on Fourth Street in New York City and that Mytton Maury, together with his ten brothers and sisters, had been brought from Virginia to New York to become Aunt Ann's "family," living at 349 Fourth Street. Here the Old Consul and Ann had settled after his lifetime of duty in England. His sons, William and Matthew, had become tobacco and cotton merchants for his import-export business traveling throughout the country. William had settled in Virginia where he and his wife had died, leaving eleven orphans for Ann to adopt.

Brief excerpts from the letters will indicate the great sense of "family" that reached across the ocean, defied the mail or communication problem, and the travel experiences. The reader will trace a deep friendship between Jefferson and James Maury that developed when they met at the Reverend James Maury's school in Shadwell, Virginia, while in their teens to just a few months before Jefferson's death.

FAMILY LETTERS

James Maury, Esq., "The Old Consul" *(1746-1840)*

In Albemarle County, near Charlottesville, Virginia, James Maury's father, the Reverend James Maury, built a little log schoolhouse in which to teach his sons. To this school came also the neighborhood boys: James Madison, James Monroe, and Thomas Jefferson.

Mr. Adams, in *The Living Jefferson*, furnishes a charming background, not only for Thomas Jefferson, but for all the boys in this group: ". . . with money, position, well-known throughout the country and socially well-connected throughout the colony, the boy could look forward to living the life of a country gentleman of that day or striving for almost any career he might choose. Meantime his father had left instructions that he should be given a good classical education, and in pursuance of the plan the lad spent the next two years studying under the Reverend James Maury, whom he later described as a 'correct classical scholar.'

"Those who had moved westward to the slopes of the Blue Ridge had been to a great extent of the best stock in Virginia. . . . There were both freedom and simplicity in the life, and a district in which in less than a hundred miles from one another such boys as Thomas Jefferson, Patrick Henry, James Madison and John Marshall were growing up simultaneously was evidently no ordinary 'frontier' or new country. . . . The men and women of this western Virginia country, establishing themselves on small or large farms, were quite capable of looking after themselves and the affairs of government, and in considering Jefferson's career and philosophy it is well to bear in mind the sort of society in which his most impressionable years were spent."

---

*Anne Fontaine Maury, *Intimate Virginiana: A Century of Maury Travels by Land and Sea* (Richmond, Va.: Dietz Press, 1941). Reprinted with permission.

This would also seem to apply to little James Maury, who grew up to be appointed by Washington to be first American Consul at Liverpool.

This unpretentious man, James Maury, with his remarkably strong personality, is best described by one of his grandsons. This anonymous clipping from an unknown magazine was among my father's papers:

My grandfather had been in business in Fredericksburg, Va., before the Revolution broke out. The continental money had ruined him. When the war was over and peace was made he thought the best way to get up was to go over to England, open an American house, receive consignments of Virginia tobacco, and ship back to the United States any goods wanted. He went to consult Mr. Jefferson, his friend from boyhood, who was then Secretary of State. My grandfather meant to go to Bristol, the chief city then in the American trade. Mr. Jefferson with his rare insight, said: "No, not Bristol, but Whitehaven or Liverpool will grow the fastest and be the best place. You had also better be the United States Consul; it has no revenue, but an American ship unconsigned will be put in your hands, and the fact that you are United States Consul will bring you commission business from your countrymen. General Washington is in the next room, and I will go in and propose to him that you shall be appointed as consul to Liverpool."

General Washington, of course, knew my grandfather quite well, approved of the appointment, and made it at once. My grandfather went to Liverpool, made a success of business there, and in his old age returned to his native land, but ever cherishing, as did his children, the kindest feeling towards the people of Liverpool. . . .

Ann, at the age of seventy, in an amazingly reminiscent mood wrote her cousin, Mrs. Sally C. M. Reid of Memphis, Tennessee, February 23, 1870:

My father was a Virginian, but his pride was much greater as a Citizen of the *United States* than it was as one of the State of Virginia. After living in England 50 years, and having there married my mother, an Englishwoman, his patriotism was as strong as the day he left . . . He was a personal friend of General Washington, of Mr. Jefferson, Mr. Madison, Mr. Adams, Mr. Monroe. With the three first named he kept up a correspondence till they died. He and I made three visits to Mr. Madison after we came to this country. My father abhorred sectional feelings—so did Mr. Madison. We were at Mr. Madison's when the first streak of secession, no bigger than a man's hand, arose. It was all talked over and I now have the memorandums of the conversations, written at night in my room, while memory was fresh.—Mr. Madison felt sure that Nullification would die out, he spoke of the many difficulties that had been overcome in bringing the old 13 States to agree to the Constitution. When my father went to England there were 13 dis-united States, and he gloried in the adhesion of all that formed the *United States.*

In my mind's eye I can see my father with the fire in his countenance, his eyes bright with emotion, speaking of the surprise in Europe that the Union should ever have been accomplished. My father was on board the Flag Ship of the Count de Grasse, the *Ville de Paris*, at the time of Lord Cornwallis's surrender. He saw the Count de Grasse kiss General Washington first on one cheek, then the other, and thirdly on the lips,—General Washington, my father was wont to say, received the salutation like "a coy damsel."

My pen is running riot as my tongue often does, yet as I have written in this vein I must tell you one more thing.— When my dear good father was in his 90th year, and Mr. Madison, about 10 years younger, were talking over the old times and the discussions as to the Constitution, etc., etc., Mr. Madison said: "Some of us were dead against having a Navy—but Jefferson said it would be unwise not to have vessels of war, for hereafter they might be needed to bring a refractory State to order." The conversation arose in consequences of South Carolina Nullification. . . .

. . . July 2, 1819, Matthew in New York heard from his mother:

My dear Matt
. . . When your father went to the office he begged me to write saying, "The poor fellow will think himself quite neglected," now lest you should take up such an idea Matt, I must tell you that Ann and myself were so persuaded that you were on your way home . . . nay, we were so possessed with the idea, we eyed everybody in the streets in the least like

you, and if there was an unusual ring at the door, we said, "Oh! maybe its Matt!" and often went to the door with a quick step. . . .

Yr truly affec Mother M. Maury

To William, who was at this time, the Fall of 1819, in New York . . . his father wrote:

. . . The Journal of your travels entertained the Fire-side in Rodney street not a little; and especially the *three in one bed.**

December 1, 1819, the Old Consul wrote to Will, then . . . at Charlestown:

. . . I feel greatly obliged by the friendly and hospitable attentions you have experienced in the good town of Boston: I notice your not mentioning the late President at Quincy: did you call?

Again to Will in July 1820:

I thank Mr. Madison for his intended consignment. I have had tobo [tobacco] from him, as well as from General Washington, while in the chair, but it happened in both cases that I had the mortification to find, in the event, if I had kept it longer, I should have made much money for them. We all say God bless you and I pray you to take care of your health.

Adieu! my dear son

Will to Ann from Boston, September 1820:

. . . I have an *elegant* Horse—he can trot 12 miles an hour and I at that rate can ride him . . . I prefer that mode of

---

*To Mrs. Anne Fontaine Maury Hirschfeld, from Merseyside County Museums: "In connection with a local scheme for putting plaques on the houses once lived in by well-known inhabitants of Liverpool, the Heritage Bureau has put a plaque on the house in Rodney Street where James Maury once lived."

travelling to any other, the advantages you possess in seeing the Country are so much greater, for all the Stage roads are carried along the ridges of stony land, therefore you always in the stages see the worst part of the country. On Tuesday I am going to a grand ball at Sam Appletons, given upon the opening of a new House which has cost him $60,000—a House warming it is called in these parts . . . Love &c in abundance

The Consul's letter of December, 1820, is addressed to William in New Orleans:

. . . The fall in the value of property which you state is indeed amazing and like the So. Sea bubble in old times. . . .

You, my son, have often seemed to repine at our having omitted speculating as you had suggested . . . I do however own to you that I once expected Cotton would have proved an advantageous speculation.

I am greatly satisfied with your zeal and industry and pleased with the results. . . . My son, take care of your health and do not ride your *Hobby too hard*: remember even Apollo sometimes unbent his bow.

Your affc. father

This letter written to Tom Maury at Midmon near the University of Virginia was written four months and a day before Jefferson's death on July 4, 1826:

Monticello Mar. 3.26

Dear Sir,

In answer to your inquiries in behalf of my antient & highly esteemed friend and classmate, James Maury, I need only say that I was born April 2, 1743, and that consequently allowing for change of style I shall be 83 years old on the 13th of the ensuing month of April. . . .

I pray you to assure him that I retain for him still all my schoolboy affections, and that his prosperity & Happiness are very dear to me.

My own health is very broken and my faculties so much impaired by age, as to prepare me to meet with welcome the hour which shall once more re-assemble our antient class, with its venerable head, his father, For yourself be pleased to accept assurance of my great esteem and respect.

Th. Jefferson

The Old Consul recollected "three score and ten years ago," writing from Liverpool, 1 June 1827: to his sister, Mrs. Elizabeth Herndon of Fredericksburg:

. . . You are right, for I did indeed feel much on hearing my antient class mate had left me the sole survivor of the five who were together somewhat more than *three score and ten years ago,* besides which, Mr. Jefferson, from that remote period down to his finally ceasing, had invariably treated me with friendly kindness, I may say in every way. In truth I used to believe & still do believe I must have been an early favorite, because, when at School, he very frequently requested my father to let me go with him to *Shadwell* of a Saturday . . . Altho' so distant it seemed as tho I had been left solitary!

In 1836, Ann wrote her cousin, A. P. Maury, Esquire, House of Representatives, Washington City, D.C.

. . . We had a large party (that is, a large one for our small mansion) on the 14th. February to celebrate the return of his birthday, on which he completed his 91st year . . . he is not yet strong enough to undertake a journey to Washington . . . even if a stronger inducement were held out than to witness the inauguration of Martin Van Buren . . . My father gave a vote in this City opposed to him & was probably the most aged who did *walk* to the Poll . . . As for me, I never am absent from him a single night . . . our house is No. 349 Fourth St., about two miles from the point at which the Steam Boat lands you. . . . [The Consul died in 1840]

The year 1848 found Sarah and William and their eleven children established at Windsor, a farm near Fredericksburg, Virginia. Sarah died of typhus fever, contracted from an infected well, 20th September 1849. Matthew wrote Ann, then on a visit in Liverpool, of their brother William's death on the 15th of October. Apparently Matthew took it for granted that Ann would come over from England at once and take care of the eleven orphaned children!—Which is exactly what she did:

Writing in 1870, when in her seventieth year to her cousin "Sally," Mrs. C. M. Reid of Nashville, Tennessee, Ann justified her state of single blessedness:

I think a happy married woman is much happier than a happy single woman. But for my part, I feel that my duty was so plain before me to take care of my good old father that it could not be mistaken. Once upon a time my mother thought I was giving my affections to some *man* & she did not want me to do so—she said to me "my *dear Annie*, if you will stay with your old father & mother while they live, God will bless you, & you will never repent it." Her words were a blessing to me & I have never repented staying single —I have always had plain, useful, home duties before me, so that there was nothing conflicting as to what was right to do. I had to take an orphan family whose minds were full of prejudice against me as you well know. Now, tho' they are mostly married they give me respect, nay more than respect, they love me as a mother might be satisfied to be loved. . . .

GENEALOGY CHART FOR MAIN CHARACTERS
MAURY

Rev. James Maury, 1717-1769. Scholar Maury ran a school in Shadwell, Virginia attended by his sons and Jefferson, Madison, Monroe, etc.

Of his children the following were important here:

Matthew, 1744. He took over his father's school.	*James*, 1746. George Washington appointed him our first CONSUL to Liverpool, England. He was the consul for forty years. Of five children three were important here.	*Richard*, 1766. He became a Tennessee farmer near his uncle, Abraham, in Franklin, Tennessee.

William, 1799. Married Sarah Mytton, AUTHOR. Had eleven children who were orphaned when William and Sarah died from typhoid in Virginia. Children adopted by Aunt Ann who took them to the home established for her father when he retired and returned to America. Address was Fourth Street, New York City.	*Matthew*, 1800. Became tobacco and cotton BUSINESSMAN in America, as did his brother, William.	*Ann*, 1803. Collected family letters. Made home for her father and adopted William's children.	*Matthew Fontaine Maury*, 1806-1873. OCEANOGRAPHER. Matthew often visited his cousins Ann and Rutson who lived in New York City.

Of these children one of the youngest was Mytton, 1839-1919.

(In 1865 *Mytton Maury* married *Virginia Draper* in New York City. This marriage united the MAURY and DRAPER families.)

GENEALOGY CHART FOR MAIN CHARACTERS

DRAPER

Christopher Draper in England

John William Draper, 1811-1882. Married Antonia Coetana de Paiva Pereira Gardner

Dr. Draper was born in England and came to the United States at the age of 21. He became Professor of Chemistry and later President of New York University. He was a PHILOSOPHER, HISTORIAN, SCIENTIST, pioneer in PHOTOGRAPHY and ASTRONOMY. He lived on Fourth Street, New York City.

Of five children three are important here:

Virginia   Henry, 1837-1882. AS-   Daniel, 1841-1931. METE-
                TRONOMER. Developed   OROLOGIST. Helped
                Draper Catalogue of Stars.   Henry build telescope at
                                             home, Hastings-on-Hudson.

        Virginia Draper   married in 1865   Mytton Maury

They had two daughters:

Antonia Coetana de Paiva   Carlotta Jauquina Maury
Pereira Maury, 1867-1952.   1874-1938.
ASTRONOMER,   PALEONTOLOGIST
CONSERVATIONIST

Dorothy Myers Peed
        Friend

ON THINKING

THOUGHT PROVOKERS
AND
SENTENCE STRUCTURE STUDY

Thinking, not growth makes manhood. Accustom yourself, therefore, to thinking. Set yourself to understand whatever you see or read. To join thinking with reading is one of the first maxims, and one of the easiest to follow.

ISAAC TAYLOR

The pleasantest things in the world are pleasant thoughts, and the greatest art in life is to have as many of them as possible.

To have thought far too little, we shall find in the review of life, among our capital faults.

J. FOSTER

The greatest events of an age are its best thoughts. Thought finds its way into action.

BOICE

Thoughts come into our lives by avenues that are left open, and thoughts go out of our minds through avenues which we never voluntarily opened.

EMERSON

Nothing was ever so unfamiliar and startling to me as my own thoughts.

THOREAU *Journal*, July 1840

My thoughts are my company.

THOREAU *Journal*, January 22, 1852

73

YOUR OWN WRITINGS

READ this page.   WRITE the paragraphs.
STUDY the section following.   FILE. Later CORRECT.

In this section you are encouraged to listen, think, write.

Preparation for these paragraphs should be a study of the section on paragraph writing beginning on page 188. Review the Thinking Chart and Paragraph Patterns. Study the examples for Patterns I to VI and compare the topic sentence which is underlined with the respective pattern. Be aware of these patterns from now on (see pages 192-95).

The information in "An American Parade," in this section, was written from notes taken during the TV program. It is included here to suggest that you select an informative TV program, take notes, and several days later write a report. If you use more than one paragraph, you can use transitional ideas between paragraphs as illustrated in "Composition Patterns."

Turn "A Glance at the Year 1840" into a paragraph. The kind of topic sentence you write will probably determine the pattern to use.

Comment on the statement that the *National Wildlife* magazine article on 500,000,000 years of life at stake includes references to many of the concerns for which you have heard many programs on public broadcasting or commercial TV.

By following the symbols in the Thinking Chart on page 126, you can now recognize each degree of thinking as you ask yourself these questions. Do you understand the derivation of most of the words (th) you have used? Is there a prefix (½th) on any word? Can you label the sentences (th) as simple, compound, complex? Underline the topic sentence (ts) of your paragraph (TH). If you have used more than one paragraph, look to see if you have any transitional ideas (xx) from one paragraph to another. Do you have a composition (TH)? Finally, following the explanation of ways to develop a paragraph, determine which of the methods you used in your paragraph about 1840.

A GLANCE AT THE YEAR 1840

(I have always wanted to take a single date, perhaps a calendar year, and discover what was happening at that time in history. The date 1840 appeared regularly in Kitchen Table Conversations, so I have used this date to perform the experiment. The result is interesting and revealing. It provides an introduction, likewise, to the following section on the Lowell Lectures in Boston.)

In the year 1840—

Dr. John William Draper perfected the process of taking pictures in sunlight by "photographing" his sister, Dorothy Draper, on the roof of a New York University building near Fourth Street. Also at the university, his colleague,

Samuel F. B. Morse, was working on his invention of the telegraph. He had recently brought to Draper from France the modified daguerreotype, attempting to use sunlight rather than artificial light in taking pictures. Nearby, at 349 Fourth Street,

Consul James Maury, at home in the United States from Liverpool, England, for ten years, passed on in his 94th year leaving his daughter,

Ann Maury. She received a letter of sympathy in her bereavement, and encouragement for the future from her cousin who had recently visited them to begin his convalesence. Now in Fredericksburg, Virginia,

Matthew Fontaine Maury continued his convalescence from his serious stage coach accident, pondered his future in the Navy, and determined to turn to writing to try to bring about necessary reforms in the Naval service. He used Harry Bluff as a pseudonym and wrote a regular column for the *Southern Living* magazine called "Scraps from the Lucky Bag." His purpose, among others, was to "fight for the education midshipmen desperately needed." He recommended "a rounded course of study to include languages, chemistry, natural history, astronomy, naval architecture, drawing, some international and maritime law, gunnery and tactics and mathematics." He wanted this to become a four-year course in an academy equal to West Point. Eventually Annapolis came to be and the West Wing of the main hall was named for him. In a few years Maury will have made a name for himself and will be asked to give a series of lectures on oceanography at the *Lowell Institute* in Boston. The first series of lectures began on January 3, 1840. The subject was geology and the lecturer, Professor Benjamin Silliman of Yale.

FROM THE LOWELL INSTITUTE LECTURE SERIES TO EDUCATIONAL TELEVISION

(Did you know that every time you tune to an educational TV station that you are sharing in the bequest of an 1830 will?)

In 1830, John Lowell, Jr., age thirty-three, drew up his will while on safari across Europe and Asia. The will established a series of public lecture courses for adult audiences. The lectures were to be given by the foremost authorities of the time in Lowell's native Boston, which he knew was hungry for lectures and books.

John Lowell died in 1836, and it was found that the will bequeathed a sum of $250,000 as a capital fund that would yield an annual budget of about $18,000. His cousin John Amory Lowell was named First Trustee of the Lowell Institute and was followed, over the years, by descendants Augustus Lowell, Percival Lowell, A. Lawrence Lowell, and Ralph Lowell. (If your mind adds poet Amy Lowell and Chief Justice Lowell to this list you are correct.) These Lowells carried out the will to the letter and also built a firm financial base so that the capital fund now amounts to $8,000,000.

Edward Weeks has written a book, which describes the institute as a "Yankee renaissance, cultural and commercial." He explains that the climate of New England makes for strong opinion and from the first, members of the colony flocked to the meetinghouse to exercise their minds. He says that "the spiritual eloquence and the argumentation of the meetinghouse were the food on which the Boston mind fed. . . . To listen, to argue, to question and to convince—this was a heritage that had crossed the Atlantic and taken root. It explains," he continues, "why the theater seemed frivolous to the thousands who, later, would turn out to hear the oratory of Edward Everett and Daniel Webster, and why the lecture was more epidemic in Boston . . . than in any other capital in the country."*

The will stipulated that there should be one course each year devoted to "the historical and internal evidence of Christianity," and that the rest of the courses should be very broad. Philosophy, natural history, the arts and sciences were also suggested.

Lt. Matthew Fontaine Maury gave one series of lectures when he was the director of the Naval Observatory in Washington where he was gathering information for his charts for sea captains; he had become an authority on ocean currents, particularly the Gulf Stream.

Over the years, the Lowell Institute, with the cooperation of neighboring colleges Harvard and Tufts, arranged for course credit and degrees to be given; two new universities became offshoots of the Lowell Institute—the Massachusetts Institute of Technology down the Charles River from Harvard and, in Boston, Northeastern University. These had to become separate entities because not one cent of the bequest could be spent for buildings; the money was solely for men of eminence who would fill the program.

In 1946, Ralph Lowell, then trustee of the institute, addressed the presidents of Boston University, Boston College, Massachusetts Institute of Technology, Northeastern University, and Tufts University regarding a cooperative project which would adapt the content of regular college courses to radio. The president of Harvard appointed Dr. Harlow Shapley, director of Harvard Observatory, to the committee to define a radio policy.

Eventually the council used Harvard's Blue Hills Observatory in Canton, the highest point of land available, on which to erect

---

*Edward Weeks, *The Lowells and Their Institute* (Boston: An Atlantic Monthly Press Book, Little, Brown and Company, 1966).

a tower and antenna. The basement of the observatory was converted into a transmitter room. Now the Boston Symphony Orchestra became a member of the council and provided a large chorus room for the all-important studio. Thus WGBH (Greater Blue Hills) came into being in 1948.

Finally the WGBH Educational Foundation was chartered as a nonprofit educational and musical corporation, using facilities not owned by the Lowell Institute. Thus the TV broadcasting venture carried out the letter of the John Lowell, Jr., will. The first program of WGBH-TV was October 6, 1951. It was the Saturday evening performance of the Boston Symphony Orchestra. In June, 1953, the WGBH Educational Fund was granted a permit as a noncommercial station on Channel 2.

Governor Edward Everett of Massachusetts eulogized John Lowell, Jr., in a special address to a packed house in Boston on December 31, 1839. He opened the first series of Lowell Institute Lectures on January 3, 1840, by introducing Yale Professor of Geology, Benjamin Silliman to the student audience. By October 6, 1951, Lowell's dream of education for the public had kept pace with Daguerre, Draper, and a host of others whose work on the TV camera and photography was now bringing educational programs to millions via PBS-TV. SO, it is the PBS channels, in cooperation with WGBH and commercial channels, that bring you educational programs, if you dial selectively.

When you enroll for a lecture series in the Lowell Institute, your expenses are minimal. In like manner, the "fee" for membership in the educational channel that brings PBS programs into your home is minimal and, for many, is a part of enjoying the TV service, knowing that you are truly sharing in John Lowell, Jr.'s will of 1830. There is also an opportunity on commercial channels to take a course by TV if you matriculate with the college giving the course, do the assigned work, and pay the fee.

Some time ago, Anne Fontaine Maury Hirschfeld gave me a china candlestick which was in Carlotta Maury's Thinking Room in her home in Yonkers, New York. This room comes to mind, now that we are considering being educated at home. Can a TV room today gain some of the importance of her Thinking Room?

True, Dr. Carlotta Maury, who received her Ph.D in paleontology from Cornell University, did research for forty years in many parts of South America, in the Caribbean, and in South Africa. She worked with various universities, led expeditions on her own, and was employed by industry. The Royal Dutch Shell Petroleum Company, for example, employed her as a conchologist to discover areas where oil might exist in the earth.

THINKING ROOMS—KITCHEN TABLES—THE LOWELL INSTITUTE—WGBH—PBS all have something in common: They provide opportunities for man to ponder and perhaps to act, "to push forward his own skill," as Dr. Jacob Bronowski says in the epigraph in the front of this book. He says this is the gift that makes man unique among the animals.

Now let us consider some of the educational programs you can view on TV.

"The Ascent of Man" is the Dr. Jacob Bronowski series of lectures that take the viewer all over the world and into every important era of history to answer the question Bronowski put to himself, "What makes man what he is?" This series, in whole or in part, has been repeated on PBS many times.

"Firing Line" with William Buckley on PBS lines up with Lowell's intention to bring to his countrymen an opportunity "to listen, to argue, to question, and to convince."

"The Adams Chronicles," on PBS, brought American history to us during our Bicentennial in a manner that both enlightened and enriched us as we sympathized with our forefathers' struggles. We came to understand historical events from our inception as a nation through to the beginning of our railroad system, as we followed generation after generation of the Adamses' contributions to America.

"An American Parade," a series of programs on CBS of which one on the Industrial Revolution brought me an understanding of how and by whom mass production began in America. The program, according to the notes that I made at the time, named three men responsible: Slater, Whitney, and Lowell. The Slater name is known in Rhode Island where the Slater

Mill, the first in America, was built on the Blackstone River. Whitney is the Eli Whitney who invented the cotton gin. The Lowell is Francis Cabot Lowell who toured England in 1813 to observe the procedure and production of English mills. (Discover what relation this Lowell is to the Institute Lowells.)

Francis Cabot Lowell went to Waltham on the Charles River when he returned from England, and there set up a series of mills of allied industries, thus establishing a self-contained factory where a bag of cotton would enter at one end and emerge as a bolt of cotton at the other. River water was the power—the Charles in Waltham and the Merrimack in Lowell.

His factory represented a new source of work. He trained farm girls in a special home where they were taught the factory job, were given opportunities to attend concerts and lectures, and were encouraged to save money and return to the farm so that other girls could take their places. The wage was $5.00 a week at a time when $1.50 was the going rate for an acre of land. (Readers who use this information to stimulate their ideas are urged to check on the accuracy of my note-taking by doing research on the subject in the library.)

By going from water power to woodburning steam power then to coal, the heartland of America was industrialized and eventually steel was produced.

Words such as the following appear in my notes and rough out a story: *House-building, architecture boom, sewing machine transformation, printing press by steam power, news from all points, travel begins, railroads are king, plows are mechanized, the McCormick reaper, immigrants begin a factory class.*

Dreams for All. At the 1876 Centennial in Philadelphia, a steam engine in Mechanics Hall provided the energy for all the machines on the grounds.

"The Belle of Amherst," on PBS, is a one-woman drama about poet Emily Dickinson which provided a rare experience for the viewer. Laughter with the poet's own laughter, empathy

and sympathy for the events in her life, and understanding of the writer's exacting work—all added up to another New England experience

"Civilisation," also called "The Frozen World," a series on Western man by Sir Kenneth Clark, is practically annual in its appearance on PBS. One wonders how much help Dr. John William Draper's *History of the Intellectual Development of Europe* was in Clark's research.

"The Restless Earth," on PBS, must be a companion production to "The Restless Sea," which I used in my English class as a means of helping students become aware of their minds at work. They were shown the film at the beginning of the term with the understanding that they would write a paragraph immediately after viewing it. They were told that the paragraph should not relate what the film was about, but rather tell the thoughts that went through the viewer's mind while watching it in an English-class setting. Utter candor in writing was solicited, since it was expected that the students would wonder what such a film had to do with English. This reaction was usual and was the means I took to prove to them that their thoughts can be captured on paper; that thoughts are words; and that they are in the back of the mind quite independent of conscious awareness.

"Leonard Bernstein at Harvard: The Unanswered Question" is a series of six programs on PBS. The series combines music, philosophy, and grammar. It is very heavy viewing, unless you are a music major, but the fascination one always had for Bernstein's Young People's Concerts is evident and powerful and is combined with the repeated theme of grammar in music. Music is a language; we say that it is international and that it speaks for everyone.

Bernstein's thesis begins with the questions he asks: What does music mean? Where does it come from? Where is it leading? To obtain his answers, he examines music the world over to test the hypothesis that there exists a worldwide, innate musical grammar. He chronicles the development of musical

language, what that language is saying below the surface,*
and what the language can tell us about the nature of the
human mind itself. The six lectures are titled: Musical Phono-
logy, Musical Syntax, Musical Semantics, The Delights and
Dangers of Ambiguity, The Twentieth-Century Crisis, The
Poetry of Earth.

The Mars Landing, seen on all Channels, had special significance
for one section of this book. In July, 1976, when the pictures
from Mars were being revealed, a friend and neighbor who
knew Antonia Maury put into words a thought which had
been in my mind. "I often wonder," she said, "what Miss
Maury would think about this outer space exploration, especially this on Mars."

"She would be filled with awe, and, at the same time, be
having a ball." I answered. Then I added more thoughtfully,
"She would glory in it; she would understand it; she would
appreciate its findings; she would see lessons in it for improving life on Earth."

Later I listed Antonia Maury's credentials to prove my comments. And I watched to see what the media would report about
scientists', editorialists', and science-fiction writers' reactions.

Antonia Maury's unique credentials for appreciating space exploration and the Mars landing, I reasoned, should be:

1. THE DRAPER CAMERA now in Smithsonian Institution
   and used to take the first picture in sunlight, an accomplishment which Draper considered proof that astronomers now
   had a NEW TOOL for study.
2. THE 1863 PHOTOGRAPH OF THE MOON taken by
   Draper and his son, possibly with the same camera.
3. HER OWN STAR STUDY based on the PHOTOGRAPH
   SPECTRUM ANALYSIS method developed by her grandfather and uncle.

---

*Noel Chomsky's *Transformational Grammar* is often referred to.
Chomsky is a professor at the Massachusetts Institute of Technology.

4. Her understanding of the GEOLOGY OF MOON ROCKS and now of MARS'S SURFACE STRUCTURE, because of her sister's work as a paleontologist.
5. Her readiness, as a scientist, to have her theories proved or DISPROVED because she had kept up her interest in her own research at Harvard and had discovered that some of her theories were incorrect.
6. Her concern for CONSERVATION OF THE SOIL ON EARTH which might, now, receive help from the knowledge acquired about Mars. (Note: "The Incredible Universe," *National Geographic*, May 1974, may well be considered a fifty-year update of Antonia Maury's work, which began in the summer of 1924 and so adds to her credentials.)

The first media report I saw quoted Ray Bradbury direct from Mission Control:

> I think the important thing to emphasize is this—that, as of today, we have touched Mars. There is life on Mars, and it's us—extensions of our eyeballs in all directions, extensions of our sense of touch, extensions of our heart and soul have touched Mars today. That's the message to look for there. We are on Mars. We are the Martians.

Carl Sagan, who is head of the Laboratory for Planetary Studies at Cornell University and a working member of the Viking team, was both practical and philosophical in his question and answer interview with *U.S. News and World Report:**

> *Q. What return would the citizens of the U.S. get from this expenditure?*
> A. I think civilizations are known in the long perspective by what they do—by the historical turning points which they initiate. We now have, because of our technology, a unique opportunity to explore our surroundings in space.

---

*From a copyrighted interview in *U.S. News and World Report* of August 30, 1976.

The practical advantages are immense, even in the medium-range time frame. The return does not come the year after you go there; it takes a little time. But the opportunity to compare our planet with other planets that have had different histories gives us a perspective on the alternative fates of worlds.

We live on a world that is structured in a certain way, and we wish to understand how to make it go in one direction rather than another. You can't experiment on it, because if you make a mistake you're in trouble—consider, for example, altering the climate. But nature has kindly provided us with natural experiments on nearby planets. By examining them we can gain profound insights into how our planet works and how to make it work better.

Human beings have been as successful as they are because of our spirit of exploration and adventure. At this point in human history, the surface of the planet Earth is fully explored. And at just this same moment, other worlds suddenly become accessible to us. I think it is in the deepest human tradition to seize that opportunity.

Finally, in January, 1977, I found, as a conclusion here, an editorial comment which seems to be exactly what Miss Maury might have said. It is a passage from the introductory editorial by Gilbert W. Grosvenor. In the January, 1977 *National Geographic* magazine he writes:

The difficulties in reaching Mars were physical, and they were overcome by the highest technology of which our society is presently capable. The results are nothing less than stunning. To look upon this rust-red alien world with the clear eyes of modern space techniques is an experience that ancient mythology reserved only for gods. Then, to probe and assess the Martian soil for signs of life, as far away as 235 million miles, so enlarges human capabilities that we must wonder why we cannot apply some of that power to problems that plague so many earthly cultures.*

"At STAKE: 500,000,000 YEARS OF LIFE." Among the "problems that plague so many earthly cultures" is conservation—

---

*Gilbert W. Grosvenor, Introductory Editorial, January 1977 issue of *National Geographic,* © National Geographic Society.

call it pollution, ecology, whatever you will. It reflects on man's "husbanding" of our Earth. There are many programs on this subject on our TV channels. But the following, from *NATIONAL WILDLIFE* magazine, with the title above so summarizes this present intellectual and material dilemma, and so adds to the theme of the sections from Conversation about Language to the Mars landing that excerpts from the article are appropriate to conclude this section.

All life depends on the non-living background of environment that envelops it. Life depends on the air, the water, the soil. . . .

It is this interdependence of individuals and species and the dependence of life upon non-life, that are the concern of ecology. . . .

Even as a primitive hunter and food-gatherer long ago, man showed signs of becoming a threat to the orderly structure of the environment. He grew intelligent enough to develop speech so that he could hunt and live in an unprecedentedly flexible and cooperative society. He developed tools—beginning with sticks and bones and going on to sharpened rocks—and these increased his power and flexibility. . . .

Then . . . early man made one technological advance that was unique—one before which no other creature could stand. He tamed fire. . . . About ten thousand years ago, came the development of agriculture and herding. Man domesticated plants and animals. He deliberately raised and cultivated those which provided milk, eggs, wool fiber, labor, food. This strained the normal balance of the environment in several ways. . . .

[The article then summarizes the effects of the Industrial Revolution, of modern medicine and hygiene, of accumulating industrial and human waste, and of population growth as they effect life on earth.]

If mankind's present rate of population increase continued for another three hundred years, man would make up about 10 percent of the total weight of animal life on Earth. The animals man feeds on and uses for various purposes would then make up almost all the rest, and wildlife would be just about totally wiped out! . . . Do we really want an earth made up of little but men and algae? . . .

We must depend on the good sense of people generally—heightened by the gathering misery—to adopt a new attitude toward childbearing, and to make a new effort to think in terms, not just of themselves, but of the entire Family of Man. Perhaps everything together can combine to edge individuals toward a clearer consciousness of the manner in which their own safety and comfort is bound to all mankind, and, beyond that, to the total environment.*

*Isaac Asimov, "At Stake: 500,000,000 Years of Life," Copyright 1972 by the National Wildlife Federation. Reprinted from the April-May issue of *National Wildlife* magazine.

ON NEWSPAPERS

THOUGHT PROVOKERS
AND
SENTENCE STRUCTURE STUDY

Newspapers are the schoolmasters of the common people—a greater treasure to them than uncounted millions of gold.

Henry Ward Beecher

The careful reader of a few good newspapers can learn more in a year than most scholars do in their great libraries.

F. B. Sandorn

I read the newspaper to see how God governs the world.

John Newton

The newspaper is one of the foremost wonders of the modern world. The family that does not take, and carefully read, at least one newspaper, is not living in the nineteenth century.

J. A. Broadus

We have the newspaper which does its best to make every square acre of land and sea give an account of itself at your breakfast table.

Emerson

YOUR OWN WRITINGS

READ this page.
STUDY the section following.

WRITE the paragraph.
FILE. Later CORRECT.

This section on newspaper reading attempts to justify the first
two quotations on the preceding page. Your first paragraph
could register your agreement or disagreement.

Write paragraphs to show that you have recognized that you
increase your knowledge and understanding dramatically when
you relate ideas to your reading.

This would be a good time to use the library to gather information related to an idea that interested you and to include
it in a paragraph demonstrating your research.

Don't forget to check your grammar and sentence structure
constantly.

Learn to use the bibliography cards shown in the back of the
book whenever you do library reference work. The habit of
recording necessary information when you first do your
reference reading and note-taking will save you emotional and
clock time in the long run.

If a copy of *Matthew Fontaine Maury: Scientist of the Sea* is
available to you, do the research suggested by items G, H, I, J
and K on the newspaper article on the Gulf Stream. Use the
card catalogue and/or other reference material if you do not
have this book. *The Periodical Index* would be a good source
of information.

READING PERIODICALS AND RELATING IDEAS

ON MOON PHOTOGRAPHY
Dr. John William Draper
scientist, philosopher, historian
Dr. Henry Draper
physician, astronomer

"Scooped" the Astronauts

FIRST PORTRAIT OF MOON'S FACE
TAKEN AT HASTINGS-ON-HUDSON*

By RUBY LITINSKY

HASTINGS-ON-HUDSON—

While most of us earthlings are still looking with awe at pictures of the moon taken by the Apollo astronauts last month, a Hastings-on-Hudson family proudly views the first photograph ever taken of the moon's face.

The first moon portrait was taken in Hastings in 1863 by Dr. Henry Draper, who, with his father Dr. John Draper, built the camera and a 15-and-a-half-inch aperture telescope to get the "closeup."

A print of the picture, signed by Dr. Henry Draper, hangs in the 271 Broadway home of his grandnephew, Dr. John Draper.

"I'm just sorry 'grandpa' isn't around to see the astronauts' pictures," Dr. Draper said, "he'd really enjoy them, they're great."

Camera in Smithsonian

The camera used by the Drs. Draper to photograph the moon is now in the Smithsonian Institution, in Washington, D.C.

However, the telescope was donated to Harvard University some years ago, and at the end of World War II was sent by Harvard to what is now Red China. None of the Drapers know

---

*From the White Plains, New York, *Reporter Dispatch*, January 1969. Courtesy of Westchester Rockland Newspapers.

its fate now, but Dr. Draper's son, John William Jr., a college teacher, admits it would be nice if somehow the family could get the telescope out from behind the Bamboo Curtain.

Dr. John Draper, who helped build the telescope and camera, is credited with taking the first portrait ever made, using his sister as a model, on March 23, 1840. He used the newly developed Daguerreotype process, which called for a 20-minute pose; and then improved the process to shorten exposure times.

Exposure Agent

His great grandson, named for him, said, "He was a chemist and realized that silver bromide was more sensitive than agents that had been used before then."

The original negative of the first moon portrait is now owned by the heirs of Sir John Herschel in England. It is on a piece of glass.

The Drs. Draper made numerous celestial photographs from an observatory they built on a hill on the side of the Hudson River specifically for their hobby.

Dr. Henry Draper, in a paper for the Smithsonian Institution published in 1864, described the location of the observatory as "on the slopes and summits of ridges of low hills, and no offensive manufactories vitiate the atmosphere with smoke.

"The advantages of the location are very great and often when the valleys round are filled with foggy exhalations, there is a clear sky over the observatory, the mist flowing down like a great stream and losing itself in the chasm through which the Hudson here passes."

Barn is Moved

Dr. John Draper's wife, Mary, said there is a family tale that the observatory was built on a rock ridge which also ran under the family barn. The constant stomping of horses created vibrations along the ridge which affected the observatory, so the barn was moved to another location on the property.

The mirrors for the telescope, which was used to photograph the moon, were ground and polished by hand by Drs. John and Henry Draper, who started their work on the project in 1858— five years before their historic picture.

This 15½-inch aperture telescope was so successful that in 1870, Dr. Henry Draper made a 28-inch aperture telescope for more pictures.

More than 1,500 pictures of the face of the moon, and of stars and the sun had been taken with the original 15½-inch instrument.

Seventeen in Night

In his 1854 report published by the *Smithsonian*, Dr. Henry Draper recalled, "On some nights, as many as 17 negatives have been taken, most of which are worthy of preservation; not less than 1,500 were made in 1862 and 1863."

The *Smithsonian* paper goes into extensive detail on how the observatory was built, its equipment created, and pictures were taken. Some fifty or so illustrations, most of them intricate diagrams, are in the report.

The observatory, which was the first ever for astrophotography, was built about 1850—and was destroyed by fire about 1918. It was located in what is now known as Draper Park.

One of the photographs of the sun, taken from the observatory by Dr. Henry Draper, established the fact that there was oxygen on the sun and thus revolutionized theories of the solar spectrum.

In 1874 the U. S. Government called on Dr. Henry Draper to organize the photographic division of the United States Commission to Observe the Transit of Venus, and for his efforts, Congress ordered a gold medal struck in his honor at the U.S. Mint in Philadelphia.

Dr. Henry Draper died in 1882, shortly after he contracted a severe cold due to exposure in a storm during a hunting expedition in the Rocky Mountains on which he estimated he had travelled 1,500 miles on horseback. He was only 45.

His father had died a year earlier.

Their camera and telescope, and Henry's photography made excellent pictures of the moon surface, especially considering that they took their pictures from the ground—240,000 miles from the moon. Craters are readily visible in the photographs and anyone who didn't know the origin of the Draper picture, might mistake it for one taken by the astronauts as they sped moonward.

The caption below the picture of the moon together with Dr. Henry Draper and Dr. John William Draper reads:

FIRST MOON portrait ever taken was made 105 years ago by Dr. Henry Draper who took the picture, at left, using a camera and telescope he and his father, Dr. John Draper, had built in their private astrophotography observatory in Hastings-on-Hudson. Admiring the picture, which clearly shows the moon's surface, are, Henry Draper of Chatham, Mass., left, and Dr. John William Draper in whose Hastings home the picture hangs. Both men are grand nephews of Dr. Henry Draper and great grandsons of Dr. John Draper.—Staff Photo by James Spencer.

ON THE GULF STREAM
Matthew Fontaine Maury
oceanographer
Dr. Daniel Draper
meteorologist

"GULF STREAM SWIRLS SPEED SHIPS, JOG WEATHER"

This headline on the column by Robert C. Cowen, which is quoted below, appeared in the *Christian Science Monitor* on July 28, 1973.* It provides an excellent opportunity for the reader to test his ability to relate his knowledge of the subject, as well as question ideas or become curious to know more. Everyone reacts according to his interests and background.

As an example of how one student reacted to this article and the one following, and as an opportunity for the reader to gain an understanding of the relation between the ocean and the weather, ideas have been noted and lettered for reference. Following the article, lettered notations are repeated to refer to specific sources of information which will make of this newspaper article a key to broader reading. This example can be multiplied many times by the inquisitive reader and seeker for broader knowledge.

Spinning like lazy merry-go-rounds, vast water masses frequently drift away from the Gulf Stream. It now looks as though they could be a boon to shipping.

Gulf Stream (A)
boon to
shipping (B)

A captain, catching the favorable current in one of these eddies, could cut half an hour off the trip between the U.S. East Coast and Bermuda. Conversely, if he unknowingly breasted an unfavorable flow, he could lose as much as forty-five minutes.

Here is a way to make practical use of the most intriguing Gulf Stream feature discovered in recent years—the cold water eddy. With diameters up to several hundred miles, these are roughly circular, rotating masses of cold northern water. They are roped in by a bit of the warmer Gulf Stream that has pinched itself off from the main flow.

feature
discovered (C)

Such eddies probably play an important, though poorly known, role in ocean circulation and weather. And that means worldwide weather, since every major ocean has its equivalent of the Gulf Stream.

ocean circulation
and weather (D)

Although they began to notice them about a decade ago, oceanographers have only realized the importance of the eddies in recent years. They are so huge, it's hard to appreciate them from a ship on the surface or even from an airplane. But seen from the perspective of a satellite, they are impressive.

perspective
of a satellite (E)

The water in an eddy can be 8 degrees F. colder than the

surrounding sea. This shows up sharply in infrared (heat) pictures taken by weather satellites. It represents an enormous energy store.

Oceanographers have found eddies that extend from the surface to the ocean floor. Last year, Philip L. Richardson, of the University of Rhode Island, found an eddy whose circulation extended downward for almost three miles. Working from the research ship *Mt. Mitchell* of the U.S. National Oceanic and Atmospheric Administration (NOAA), he estimated that size of eddy alone could involve a water volume equal to twenty days' Gulf Stream flow past Cape Hatteras.

Since that flow equals the flow of several thousand Mississippi Rivers, an eddy's mass and energy must be vast.

In the atmosphere, energy represented by temperature differences between different air masses powers much of our weather. Moreover, it expresses itself in eddies that form along warm and cold fronts between the air masses. These are the cyclonic storms, hurricanes, and typhoons.

This is why oceanographers are so intrigued with the Gulf Stream eddies. As a conference at Britain's Royal Society concluded three and one half years ago, such eddies may be as important to the "weather" of the sea as blizzards and cyclones are to weather in the air above. And they may even influence

pictures taken   (F)

energy represented
by temperature
differences   (G)

conference
at Britain   (H)

that atmospheric weather as well.

Ocean scientists have only begun the detailed studies needed to understand whether and to what extent this may be the case. Meanwhile, canny shipmasters may profit from knowledge already in hand, as suggested by NOAA's Dr. Alan A. Strong. He notes that easily obtained satellite pictures could supplement sailing charts by outlining the position of eddies so sailors could take advantage of their flow.

sailing charts   (I)

This adds a space-age footnote to the tool Ben Franklin gave to sailors when he discovered the Gulf Stream in the eighteenth century.

Benjamin Franklin   (J)

Gulf Stream   (K)

"WEATHER SATELLITE LAUNCHED"

VANDENBERG AFB, Calif. (AP)—A three-stage Delta rocket shot aloft Sunday with a 230-pound satellite vehicle designed to televise daily picture coverage of the world's weather.

Called Essa 3, the 22x42-inch hatbox-shaped spacecraft was aimed at a polar orbit 865 miles high which would take it around the Earth once every 113 minutes.

The launch, at 3:39 A.M., was the first on the West Coast by a Delta rocket, made up of a Thor missile with three solid rockets strapped on its sides for extra thrust and topped by two smaller stages. Deltas have orbited 37 satellites from Cape Kennedy.

The satellite is the third of a series named for the Environmental Science Services Administration (ESSA) of the Department of Commerce. Two earlier Essas were launched last February.

Essa 3 carries two cameras, either of which can meet the goal of photographing weather all over the world once each day. One camera is to be kept in reserve while the other operates.

The photographs are to be stored on magnetic tape and radioed on command to ground stations.

The craft also carried sensors to measure the solar heat energy available to keep the Earth's atmosphere in motion, creating storms and winds.

(Sun Sentinel, October 3, 1966)

Reading in Depth

While it is true that Ben Franklin gave "a tool" to sailors when he discovered the Gulf Stream in the eighteenth century, it is likewise true that Matthew Fontaine Maury is considered the Father of Oceanography. A dictionary lists the two as follows: Benjamin Franklin, 1706-1790, American statesman, scientist, inventor, writer. Matthew Fontaine Maury, 1806-1873, father of oceanography.

Most of the following references are from *Matthew Fontaine Maury, Scientist of the Sea* by Frances Leigh Williams, published by Rutgers Press. This book will intrigue anyone who is interested in reading American history from the point of view of people rather than events. It should be in every library. More than two hundred pages of notes and bibliography will give you an excellent example of careful documentation.

Reference to the Maury-Draper Genealogy Chart in this book, pages 70-71, will disclose Matthew Fontaine Maury, the oceanographer; Sarah Mytton Maury (Mrs. William Maury) whose interview with Maury for her book *The Statesmen of America in 1846* is described in the Williams book on page 166.

Four chapters in *Scientist of the Sea* are referred to in particular: Chapter VIII, "Scientific Opportunity at Last"; Chapter IX, "Superintendent of the United States Naval Observatory"; Chapter X, "Charting the Winds and the Currents"; Chapter XI, "For Scientific Cooperation Between Nations"; Chapter XIII, "The Physical Geography of the Sea"; Chapter XVI, "Crusade for a United States Weather Bureau." Other interesting reading would include the chapter (XII) on the Atlantic cable which describes Maury's work with Samuel Morse and Cyrus Field. Other sources are marked accordingly.

Notation	*Subject*	*Reference*
(A)	Gulf Stream	Williams: pages 260, 261
(B)	boon to Shipping	Williams: page 184-190
(C)	feature discovered	Williams: page 148 ff.; also page 535
(D)*	ocean circulation and weather	Williams: pages 309-326
(E)	perspective of a satellite	*Sun-Sentinel*, October 3, 1966
(F)	pictures taken	*The Reporter Dispatch*, see page 89.
(G)	energy represented by temperature differences	Williams: pages 180 ff.
(H)	conference at Britain	Williams: pages 205-224

---

*Though the comprehensive weather service that Maury envisioned in 1861 did not come into being until about 1870, inventions and events had taken place, by 1966, which would make the kind of weather forecasting referred to in (E) a possibility.

Today, in Central Park, New York City, at Seventy-ninth Street and Transverse Road, is the castlelike weather tower, called the Belvedere. Here weather conditions are recorded twenty-four hours a day, and broadcasts such as "Central Park readings" are familiar to city dwellers. The New York Metropolitan Bureau is one of the oldest institutions of its kind in the United States, and it is a museum as well.

Of note is the first automatic device for recording rainfall. It was made by Dr. Daniel Draper (see Genealogy Chart) who was a naval engineer when he began weather recording at the Central Park Arsenal. The instrument consisted of a bucket, used as a collector on the roof, and a tube through which the water ran into a second bucket in Dr. Draper's office. When the bucket was full, it tipped, making a record on paper.

(I)   sailing charts   Williams: pages 150 ff.
       (Look for the
       Maury name on
       sailing charts today)

(J)   Benjamin Franklin   Williams: see Index under
                                    Bache, Alexander Dallas,
           and   who is the great grandson
                                    of Franklin. Many references
(K)   Gulf Stream

Reading in Depth—
A Research and Writing Experience

Using the following dates, the reader can develop an interesting report on the development of photography as astrophotography and conclude with the following 1935 information: during World War II, the Draper telescope went behind the Bamboo Curtain for scientific study.*

1840	1854
1850	1858
1863	1874
1864	1882
1870	1918

In 1935 Harvard Observatory, now a branch of the Smithsonian Institution, published Antonia Maury's eleven-year study of Beta Lyra, a binary star. This was the first star study using the astrophotography method developed by the Drapers, father and son (her grandfather and uncle), and was considered basic in the fast developing field of astrophysics. For the next fifteen years Miss Maury made at least yearly visits to the observatory to learn the developments of her study. She did not always find that her theories were correct.

---

*Though these dates relate to *Matthew Fontaine Maury: Scientist of the Sea* by Frances Leigh Williams, cited above, general reference sources would also give necessary information.

ON SCIENCE AND CULTURE

THOUGHT PROVOKERS
AND
SENTENCE STRUCTURE STUDY

Our new knowledge of the atom also brings us new hope for a deeper understanding of ourselves and of our world problems. For the same experiments which are giving us atomic power are also giving us atomic vision; we can look inside the atom and see that there is something there beyond the material. We can see through to a new horizon of the spirit.

Dr. Donald H. Andrews
Distinguished Professor of Chemistry

Should we find that our complicated social structure can be regarded as simply as one of the atoms in an infinitely great cosmos which we know scientifically to exist, is it not possible that, as we develop our mental processes, we may become more mature? Perhaps man can even develop a spiritual attitude to the point where he can think of himself objectively and say, "Man, you have been silly—silly in your behavior toward your fellowman. Why aren't you as well integrated as all of the well-integrated creations of which you are a part?"

Dr. Armand Spitz, from a Palm Beach Round Table
Lecture, Palm Beach, Florida

No man has lived who has not known the charm of great music or great art, or the sparkle of a brook in the springtime, or the thrill of the honk of geese on a still night over a busy city; or who has not known the thrill of standing on a mountain top or the subtle satisfaction of great literature.

Dr. Vannevar Bush, from *Two Cultures*

YOUR OWN WRITINGS

READ this page.
STUDY the section following.

WRITE the paragraphs.
FILE. Later CORRECT.

In the quotations on the preceding page, do both Dr. Andrews and Dr. Spitz prove Dr. Bush's quoted statement, and his denial on page 106 that the two types of culture will never meet? Explain in detail and add your opinion.

Note the date (1963) when Dr. Bush, whom President Truman appointed to the Manhattan Project in World War II, made these statements to a college graduation class. Find the paragraphs beginning, "True, it is difficult . . ." and "And yet . . . " to compare with events today. Would reaction to these paragraphs vary according to age? Why? Give details.

You are a vocational student, an industrialist, a mechanic, etc. How can you embrace the two cultures Bush talks about? Should you, in order to "make a life of success into a life that is full and happy?" Explain.

Have the paragraphs you have written for this section shown improvement in construction and in your ease in writing?

Label your paragraphs by pattern number, also the development used. See pages 192 to 195.

With reference to page 9, Working Tools, have you found a good Critic/Reader/Corrector to assist you in your self-study? I hope so.

FACE TO FACE WITH SPACE*

by Armand Spitz

In the few years since man has been intelligently space conscious, and has been doing something about it, he has been forced to come face to face with new ideas, new concepts; he has found that each time he achieves a goal, another goal opens out before him. Each time he fails in any portion of his program, he is compelled to chalk it up to experience, to learn from his failure, and to try again. Never before in history have men been forced to conduct such intricate experiments in the full glare of publicity, and with the not-always-tolerant public almost breathing down the scientists' necks.

This morning, as I was driving to Palm Beach, I heard that Echo II, the big space balloon, which would have been as high as a fourteen-story building, had just, a few hours ago, broken up in space. And instead of becoming the brightest non-astronomical object in the sky, had come down in a shower of gleaming particles. I don't know what happened. The people who launched Echo II don't know what happened. It was simply an experiment that failed. However, from it we will probably learn how to make later experiments successful. Being face to face with space forces us to recognize that successes and failures are all part of the program.

With all of its complexities, it's hard to speak of the space effort in logical terms: either chronological or technological. There are so many intermarriages of disciplines in the overall space effort, so many Terpschorean advances, retreats and side-steps that our sophistication is leading us to patience, even though impatience is more easily felt. This is an achievement that hasn't come easily, nor will it be easy in the face of spectacular achievements by those to whom we would prefer to feel superior. In discussing this subject, it would be gratifying if it were possible to have an orderly flow of ideas. Instead of this, we must be content in random jumpings from the knowledge we gain from today's successes or failures to the hypothesis of the past or to the guess-

---

*Courtesy Mrs. Armand Spitz, widow of the late Dr. Armand Spitz. "Face to Face with Space" was a lecture delivered to the Palm Beach Round Table, Palm Beach, Florida, January 15, 1962.

work of the future. It's a reality that every minute of our lives is fraught with excitement. Reality is, in fact, out-fictioning Buck Rogers, who was the only articulate spokesman for space in the antiquity of a few years ago.

As man has attemped to reach out, he has had to expand his horizons quite literally. When he first saw the moon, perhaps from the protection of his cave at night, he did not say, "That's the moon." You must remember that he wasn't the Intelligent Individual that you and I are today. You and I have inherited a great cultural tradition; but our ancestors, anthropologically speaking, may have taken hundreds or thousands of years to get the concept of moon in their minds. Without thinking, they watched it change in shape and position from night to night, and, after some centuries of this, these two-legged creatures began to *think*. When they began to *think*, they became men. Before that, they were simply some sort of anthropoid creatures, but they were not entitled to be called men at all. When they began to *think* they became bigger. They gained courage and more inquisitiveness. If there is anything that marks the divine spark of man, it is probably the drive to gain knowledge and to understand what he is learning. This is what has kept man always striving outward. No matter how far out we reach in the exploration of space, there will always be more space to be explored. As the unknowns become known, more unknowns arise.

Our ancestors looked at the moon, they looked at the stars, they reached out into the space beyond the stars. But could they chart space? Hardly! Men like Copernicus and Galileo were simply admitting to their minds the preliminary concepts which would act as springboards, from which they could learn a little more, and then a little more than that; man is still in the same process today.

Men invented new tools to help them observe, and created mathematics to help interpret the observations. They built observatories. Then they built new sciences on the basis of the observations with telescopes, the photographs which they made, and the hissing static they learned to hear.

When, only a few years ago, the National Science Foundation decided to build a great new astronomical observatory at a spot which might be free from the lights of civilization for a long period of time, they selected Kitt Peak near Tuscon. This mountaintop, ideally located astronomically, meteorologically, and culturally was on ground belonging to the Papagos Indians. It was sacred ground, and the tribal council didn't want its reservation defiled. Finally, an astronomer in Tucson invited the Papagos tribal council to come to the observatory when there was a bright half-moon in the sky. With the aid of an interpreter, the astronomer explained that all they wanted to do was reach out to the heavens so they could understand them better. The tribal council adjourned and came back with the decision that "the men with long eyes" might use the mountain top.

Man has been developing these long eyes for 350 years. He makes rainbows out of starlight and determines what stars are made of and how hot they are, and what is the state of the atoms up there, and whether they are moving toward or away from us, and how fast. The camera made possible time exposures. Then picture after picture led to the motion-picture camera and actions too fast to observe could be slowed down or frozen, or motions too slow to observe could be speeded up. When telescope and camera and spectroscope are combined, the product is called a spectroheliokinematograph—a highbrow way of saying a movie machine which takes pictures of the spectrum of the sun.

If man has learned from the use of long eyes, he has also learned from the creation of big ears. There is a relatively new discovery called radio, with which the world is familiar as a mass communications media. When a radio or television set is turned on but is not turned to a specific signal, there is a hissing noise which can always be heard. This, it is now known, comes from space, and with the aid of radio telescopes, man has been able to extend his knowledge of the universe by scores of times. As man reaches out further into space, he comes face to face with things that really exist. He gets beyond and above the interferences which make observing difficult. He launches balloons or sends instrument-carrying satellites into the heavens and, thus, adds to his store of knowledge.

As we reach out with our telescope eyes and radio ears, our minds expand to encompass these great things. But it is not only the macrocosm that we can explore. We reach out and simultaneously, dig down and reach in. With microscopes we study the structure of the molecule. With harnessed electrons we learn the structure of matter. There was a time when the word atom meant what its name implies: an indivisible particle. But now we know that the atom isn't indivisible at all, that there are electrons and protons and neutrons and positrons and neutrinos and a vast array of particles in an atom that were never dreamed of before.

So, you see, our minds must expand to comprehend these infinitesimally small things, too. Our minds must be capable of going from the microcosm where the concepts are so small they can hardly be imagined, to the macrocosm, where the concepts are so big they can hardly be imagined. You and I are in a relatively neutral vantage point, halfway between the atom and the universe.

The human race is very, very young. All of recorded history can be compressed into a very few thousand years. It is only three and one-half centuries since the first telescope was turned to the sky; less than half of a century since the radio noises from space began to bring us information. The child who was born when man launched his first satellite is just getting started in school. How young we are! Aren't we supreme egotists to think that answers should be available to us right away? Can't we see the privilege that is ours to be part of the searching process? I know we are all impatient. But to my mind, the mere fact that man is doing what he is doing means that he is fulfilling his basic intellectual goal.

Will the answers come to the questions which man proposes when he has gained the answers to earlier questions? As a matter of fact, have we any knowledge that such answers actually exist? May it not be possible that the illuminating knowledge and understanding may be delayed until long after human scientific inquisitiveness has died? Who can tell? Man, being mortal, holds it within his power to destroy himself. Will his divine spark of curiosity or his integrity or his spiritual maturity enable him to rise above the vicissitudes which are bound to face the race as it comes face to face with space?

And where are we going? We have been thinking of looking out into space and down into matter. We have learned that matter, in its elemental form, has characteristics which are not at all unlike those of outer space. As a matter of fact, our solar system, Sun, Mercury, Venus, Earth, Mars, Jupiter, Saturn, Uranus, Neptune, Pluto, and comets and meteoroids and astroids—this whole complex, as big as we think it is in terms of the earth or in terms of the atom—may simply be an atom in a meta-meta-galaxy beyond the reach of any instrument we now have or can conceive. If this be true, just where are we?

Perhaps an analogy would help. Here we are in Palm Beach, Florida, and some 3,000 miles away is San Francisco, California. I will be there soon and in order to get there, I will be traveling west across the country, but I can go to San Francisco another way. I could head east, across the Atlantic Ocean, across Europe and Asia, and across the Pacific Ocean. See, I can reach this destination by going in either of two directions which are opposite to each other. Here I am, with one hand pointing west to San Francisco and with the other pointing east to San Francisco. This is a little odd, isn't it? But really, it isn't! We know that the earth is round; hence, if I point to San Francisco with both hands, each is actually pointing beyond San Francisco and my hands are pointing to each other.

Now we are reaching a point where we must accept the conclusion which Einstein and other modern mathematicians and physicists and philosophers have reached, that space is curved. So, if I point up, I will be pointing to our atmosphere and the stars beyond, and the space beyond the stars, and the space beyond the space beyond the stars, and the space beyond that. Or, if I point down, I will be pointing to the earth, through the earth, to the atmosphere above our antipodal cousins, and the space beyond the stars beyond the space which exists for them. We may find the space way up here and the space way down there is the same space. In other words, when we look into space, we may be looking at the back of our necks.

Should we find that our complicated social structure can be regarded as simply as one of the atoms in an infinitely great cosmos which we know scientifically to exist, is it not possible that, as we develop our mental processes, we may become more mature? Perhaps man can even develop a spiritual attitude to the point where he can think of himself objectively and say, "Man, you have been silly . . . silly in your behavior toward your fellowman . . . why aren't you as well integrated as all of the well-integrated creation of which you are a part?" Perhaps, by thinking this way, we can learn a little more about ourselves, reaching out to reach in, ultimately attaining that old Socratic goal of knowing ourselves. Then it isn't impossible that man may come closer to himself in recognizing the capability and privilege which are his. He may even come closer to living with his fellowman in common sense and harmony.

This may be a dream. It is my prayer. Stranger things than this have happened in the name of science.

TWO CULTURES*

by Vannevar Bush

. . . The mission of this University, like that of every university, is to teach, or more broadly, to inculcate in a group of youth a true culture. There has been a good deal of discussion of this

---

*Courtesy Dr. Vannevar Bush and *Tufts Alumni Review* (Summer, 1963).

in recent years and there have been assertions that there are two types of culture that will never meet. I would deny this vehemently.

There is one type of culture from the standpoint of what we learned here and elsewhere for the purpose of success in the professions or in business, and there is another and deeper culture which has nothing to do with usefulness or utilitarianism. In this connection I'd like to quote a little saying made by John Burchard a few days ago to the effect that M.I.T. today was trying to humanize the sciences, and Harvard was trying to simonize the humanities. I think that at this institution we have no such quandary, for here throughout the years the two types have gone ahead hand in hand and it takes no new move to bring them together.

The culture that I speak of first is that which may be defined as the basis of wisdom, the basis of wisdom in regard to the things of this world, the basis of wisdom which will lead to success in the professions or in business. This culture has to do first with things and second with men. It is the understanding of things we mean when we speak of science, and it is the understanding of men that we mean when we speak of all those subjects which we group under the liberal arts and the humanities. Both of these have grown to the point where it is difficult indeed for a youngster in these days to grasp them fully. Furthermore, there is the danger of superficiality, and also the danger that a man who is fascinated with science will ignore and neglect that equally important aspect of his learning which has to do with the ways of men. It is equally dangerous for a man who is enamored of history and literature or poetry or the humanities generally to forget that the world is going forward at an accelerated pace in developing an intricate science which will mold our lives whether we like it or not. So, I look forward on this campus to a marrying of these, to an equal attention to the two, an attention which will inculcate in every youth who graduates here a respect for, a knowledge of, a liking for the matter of things in this world, and an equal liking for the matter of the organization and interrelationship of men in their civilization.

True, it is difficult for any man to keep up with science as it proceeds today at an accelerated rate. We see today more scientists in the world working than there have been before in the entire history of humankind, and we see advances in science made so rapidly that it is almost impossible to keep up with them. We see a public enamored of things that are not science at all but applied engineering, and enamored of the trivialities and the spectacular, while the great advances in science go almost un-noticed. Take for example the thing that is going on today all about us, the unraveling, the decoding, the interpretation of the genetic code (see *Life* magazine for October 4, 1963) which determines from the arrangement of genes on a chromosome and their individual characteristics the entire development of a human organism. One of the most dramatic, one of the most exciting searches that has ever occurred in human science, in our whole search for the truth over generations.

And yet that is almost unnoticed in the midst of the hurrah about shooting a shot at the moon. And in all science things are going ahead, affecting not merely our lives, our way of living, our standards, our gadgetry, but also our philosophy and the way in which we look at the world. Take for example the indetermi-nation principle, the multiplication of elementary particles in the hands of the physicists, the whole question of relativity, the spec-ulations about negative time, the expanding universe, the colliding galaxies, the evolution of stars, the probability of millions of planets that are inhabitable throughout the cosmos. These things stretch our imagination and broaden our outlook. And one can turn also to the ideas of man and the understanding of man and see an equally spectacular advance and an equally kaleido-scopic change, with the rise of nationalism, the end of the domi-nance of a race, the beginning of the struggling of democracy in lands that are by no means ready for democracy, perhaps the end of great wars; at least a stalemate as two great powers look at each other and pull back and temporize, as two scorpions will temporize if you put them in a box where they may fight but where if they get in the position where each can sting the other they will withdraw. We may be seeing the end of great wars; at least we are seeing an utter change in all of men's inter-relationships one with another.

It is an exciting time in which to live, and my hope is that this university will continue to inculcate in the young students who come here the love of knowledge, a keen passion to know things and to know men, that they may go forward with culture, with the basis for wisdom in regard to their own professional careers and in regard to the decisions which they make as citizens.

I have spoken of culture in the utilitarian sense, as the practical basis of wisdom for success in professional life or in business. There is another culture which has nothing to do with utilitarianism. It can never be taught, but it can be exemplified. Parts of it rest on a technique, and that can be taught. But that culture itself can only be absorbed by living in an atmosphere of culture, the culture that reaches beyond material success in this world, that stretches out to acquire from living in a hectic world not only success, not only satisfaction from the proper carrying on of a career, but the happiness which comes only to a full life.

No man has lived who has not known the charm of great music or of great art, or the sparkle of a brook in the springtime, or the thrill of the honk of geese on a still night over a busy city; or who has not known the thrill of standing on a mountain top or the subtle satisfaction of great literature.

I would see in this university then two cultures, one aimed at creating among the men and women who come here the basis for success in their lives, in their contribution to the society of which they will become a part. But beyond this, by exemplification and by the atmosphere in which they live, I would see the absorbing of a culture which transcends all of this; which and which only can make a life of success into a life that is full and happy.

The Winter, 1964, *Tufts Alumni Review* carried an article entitled "A Ransom of Greatness" which indicated relationships uniquely interesting here. In January, 1964, in a White House honor ceremony, President Johnson presented the National Medal of Science to Dr. Bush "for distinguished achievements in electrical engineering in the technology of computing machines . . ." and a similar medal to the Father of Cybernetics, the late Dr. Norbert Wiener, "for marvelously versatile contributions profoundly original, ranging within pure and applied mathematics, and penetrating boldly into the engineering and biological sciences." Dr. Brush and Dr. Wiener took their first college mathematics with a venerable professor, Dr. William Ransom, who was also an astronomer and friend of Antonia Maury and Dr. Harlow Shapley. He was my honored professor and friend.

ON POETS AND PHILOSOPHERS

THOUGHT PROVOKERS
AND
SENTENCE STRUCTURE STUDY

Emerson is our nineteenth-century poet most in need today of being rediscovered.

Hyatt H. Waggoner

Ideas control the world.

Garfield

He [Thoreau] would remind us that "a man is rich in proportion to the number of things he can do without"; that the faculty of thought, or the ability to contemplate one's self and the grandeur of the universe, give us deeper satisfaction and pleasure than most material wealth.

Wade Van Dore

My dissertation was an in-depth study of the struggle of one person (the poetic genius, Emily Dickinson) to bridge the gap between modern scientific developments and the goal of the humanities: the ability to see life whole.

Emma J. Phillips

First about Thoreau: I like him as well as you do. In one book [Walden] he surpasses everything we have had in America. You have found this out for yourself without my having told you; I have found it out for myself without your having told me. Isn't it beautiful that there can be such concert without collusion? That's the kind of "getting together" I can endure.

Robert Frost, in a letter to Wade Van Dore*

---

*From *Selected Letters of Robert Frost* edited by Lawrance Thompson. Copyright © 1964 by Lawrance Thompson and Holt, Rinehart and Winston, Publishers.

READ this page.   WRITE the paragraphs.
STUDY the section.   FILE. Later CORRECT.

Do you have to be told that Wade Van Dore is a poet after reading "The Language and Message of *Walden*"? Why? Include words, phrases, sentences that appeal to you in your paragraph response.

What statement by or about Thoreau impressed you in "New Bust in the Hall of Fame"? How? Why?

Can you picture Concord neighbors Emerson and Thoreau chatting casually? Which one would you enjoy visiting with? Why?

Emily Dickinson says again and again, in the dramatization *The Belle of Amherst*, "Now that's a word to tip your hat to." She always had pad and pencil at hand to capture words and ideas as they came to mind. As a poet, words were, literally, her stock in trade; so, too, are words to the newspaper reporter. Compare and contrast these two types of artisans with words.

In "A Summary of a Dissertation," check off the sentences that you consider topic sentences for long and detailed portions of the dissertation. Is this summary, then, made up of topic ideas? Is this one reason why you probably had to read the page several times to understand the message? Explain.

*   *   *

If you intend to do college-level work, now is the time for you to study the last section of this book.

Turn to page 210 and read carefully No. 5 of "Preparing the Formal Paper." You will see that already certain paragraphs in the last Conversation—here called by the Latin word Colloquium—have been called to your attention and that the transitionals between paragraphs help give the entire paper unity.

You will note that the style is more scholarly than any other writing in the book. For this very reason, a study of the vocabulary, sentence structure, and paragraphing can all become a review, as if for a final test; at least it will measure your understanding of good writing.

ON THOREAU

NEW BUST IN THE HALL OF FAME*

by Wade Van Dore

Rather sadly, I thought, Henry David Thoreau recorded in his all-important journal that his friend and neighbor Emerson was a little too dignified, a little too much the gentleman to "trundle" a wheelbarrow through the streets of Concord.

Should we, then, along with Thoreau, say "alas" to Emerson's lack of assertiveness with a wheelbarrow? Is any man who observes the dictates of convention and fashion not reaching toward his potential of true greatness? Is he not quite noble, say, if he spends precious time selecting a necktie to match a selected suit? If he makes frequent trips to the neighborhood barber? Prickly Thoreau affirmed by his every word and action that any man who subscribes to frivolity of any description (except, of course, playing with children and kittens) is not on the path to greatness.

After an accountable, we could say loaded, delay, this scorner of mores and etiquette who brought humble Walden Pond to the attention of the entire literate world finally has been elected to the Hall of Fame, thus setting up a situation which is puzzling, intriguing. I suspect this appointment came about largely through the honors bestowed upon his memory in recent years by India, it now being conceded that Gandhi's unique, stupendous program gained its initial impetus through his reading of Thoreau's heretofore almost unnoticed essay *Civil Disobedience*—or, as it is sometimes called, *On the Duty of Civil Disobedience*. It is said that Gandhi later took Thoreau's books to jail with him for sustainment.

I must admit that I was very surprised at this election, for perhaps no other writer has been more critical of the average American's manner of living, and of governmental procedure. Did somebody "slip up"? To reconcile or correlate his opinions, his whole life that had such an elemental tang to it, with the so-called American Way would—to use a current expression—"take some doing."

---

*Reprinted by permission from *The Christian Science Monitor*, 1967 The Christian Science Publishing Society.

Rather paradoxically, he might be called the most American as well as the least American of our writers, being thoroughly American in the old traditions of prudence, common sense and aspiration, but unAmerican in lacking that capacity which most Americans seem to have in great measure, the ability to tolerate any form of sloth, waste or pretense. So scornful was he of deviousness in either low or high places that he bragged, at least to his journal, that he never read a president's speech. Being impatient with people sympathetic yet reluctant to lend a practical hand toward the abolishing of slavery, he broke the law by helping Negroes along the underground railway, and by refusing to pay his taxes, thereby getting himself into jail, and thereby writing his now famous paper on civil disobedience.

Thoreau was indeed a super-individualist who practiced free enterprise and free speech almost as no one had ever done before or has done since. He was a non-voter through conviction, not laziness, and this fact alone could have eliminated him from the Hall. Were the electors aware of this? Were they aware that when he lectured in the basement of a New England church he said he hoped he'd helped to undermine it? Surely an election to the Hall of Fame would seem to imply some sort of an endorsement of the person so honored. Or can it possibly be that the electors mean now to elect nominees who become famous, or notorious, totally ignoring the qualifications previously required? However this may be, some of the new readers of *Walden* and *Civil Disobedience* are going to have a hard time reconciling this man's so pointed life and words with prevalent lax practices.

If Thoreau were here now, he would challenge our "economy of abundance treadmill," as someone has called it, with his dear creed of scarcity. He would repeat what he said a hundred years ago that "things are in the saddle and ride mankind," and passionately urge us to "simplify, simplify, simplify." He would remind us that "a man is rich in proportion to the number of things he can do without"; that the faculty of thought, or the ability to contemplate one's self and the grandeur of the universe, gives us deeper satisfaction and pleasure than material wealth.

Using the term "wealth" in this connection now seems a little too dignified to apply to a great part of our material accumulations which, almost everyone will agree, are mere gadgets and trash. For a time some of us thought that America's staggering output of cheap merchandise was Russia's secret weapon, but now it appears that Russia and practically all nations are trying to match us in this department.

If Thoreau could visit a present-day American household, I feel sure he would, after painstakingly noting its functioning, proclaim that the greatest danger of this time is not the hydrogen bomb, nor distrust between nations, but, to use the word inclusively as he used it, the above mentioned *things* which from once being only an annoyance to wiser folk, have slowly, insidiously, become the Great American Burden! Adults have become like small children we have noticed at Christmastime, who, becoming confused and irritated and finally exhausted by too many new toys, often escape from them to a quiet corner where they can renew their playing with some old, familiar dear treasure of several Christmases back.

But what if after all the electors of Thoreau really knew what they were about! This is not impossible. Perhaps they are now secretly hoping that readers will pass over his extreme political and social views and grasp his great message of simplicity, the subject really nearest his heart. Perhaps they realize as many of us do, that if we are indeed in a treadmill-trap of the "economy of abundance," it is high time a mass movement was started to help get us out of it.

But coming back to Emerson and the wheelbarrow—this homely useful object could stand as a symbol of the difference which persisted between these two men. Both were lofty thinkers and their friendship was certainly on a lofty, albeit practical, level. But there were gnats up there. While each had character enough to stock a village, each felt a certain irritant in the other. Emerson grew annoyed more than once at Thoreau's extreme alertness and vigor in all his mental and physical doings. He seemed to think his friend was overtrained for the battle of life—Thoreau did speak in *Walden* about "driving life into a corner" as if it were an antagonist—that his blows of rhetoric and his tricky paradoxes were not quite warranted. Thoreau on the other hand was definitely not pleased with that quality of *gentlemanness* in Emerson.

Yet at the end, Emerson, surviving the sage of Walden Pond, said this about his friend: "Thoreau gives me, in flesh and blood and pertinacious Saxon belief, my own ethics. He is far more real, and practically obeying them, than I. The country knows not yet, nor in the least part, how great a son it has lost. . . . His soul was made for the noblest society. . . . Wherever there is knowledge, wherever there is virtue, wherever there is beauty, he will find a home."

Those who visit the Hall of Fame and see the new bust

may notice the last three short sentences of *Walden* inscribed beneath it, and be re-reminded of a need for a wakeful alertness in the world situation as in a personal sense. Beyond the most cultured bickering about politics, nationalism, religion, and even Thoreau's unique cult of simplicity itself, eloquently and hopefully these lines say: *Only that day dawns to which we are awake. There is more day to dawn. The sun is but a morning star.*

THE LANGUAGE AND MESSAGE OF *WALDEN**

by Wade Van Dore

Light adding to light, facets of brilliance encircling a bold design; exactness poised in yellow of New England gold; words decorating life, sentences offering ferny paths through limitless labyrinths of human inclination and direction.

This was the language and the message of *Walden* that long ago touched the imagination of a boy. *Walden* was a sky that offered the faculty of soaring to all poetry. *Walden* was a book that tendered the earth's act of dew and its clear veins of rivers to every human thirst. *Walden* was a resting point amid a cluster of openings as valid as stars, a statement by one who had pierced to the core of man's conception of reality. The pages or leaves of the book seemed akin to tree leaves, fern leaves; yet its language appeared to have been gathered by the crystal-principle— that beautiful law we can see in operation in winter's garden when frostferns grow upon our window glass.

How does a writer find his way through the infinite possibilities of language? Thoreau took his words afield and exposed them to all the polished elements of nature. He honored them with sunlight, pronounced them in the presence of rocks, colored them with a dye of dandelions, dipped them into the high, musical response that a pine tree makes when stroked by traveling winds.

Life must supply words with power that is able to sustain life. Thoreau sharpened his life the way anyone can sharpen a pencil. He did this in order to be able to use edged words when challenging soggy thinking habits of men. For he had decided

---

not to be a blur, a human abstraction in an intricate world order that might seem to countenance followers of abstraction. He wrote: "If words were invented to conceal thought, then printing is a great improvement on a bad invention."

Anyone can muddy up an idea with words, then conceal himself in it. Thoreau determined to approach old and newly discovered ideas or propositions as if they were uncut diamonds, then with strokes of words carve them until all their beauty stood revealed. To do this would require the shaping and tempering of his own self, for one cannot cut diamond with chalk. Diamond cut diamond. Yet brilliance was not everything. So, with the image of clarity ever in mind, he resolved to be not only a cutting tool or a ready thorn, but a puckering flavor, a tip-tone of sound, an antenna raised high to detect all the world's tremblings of feeling.

How fortunate that we have the crop of words harvested by this writer safely stored in the bins of books. The actual sparkling waters of Walden Pond cannot match the territory cooled by *Walden*, the book. This is a kind of giant metaphor that bridges what many regard as a gulf between man and nature. It is also a new form of poetry: we once had stanza verse, blank verse, free verse; now we have Walden verse which, with pacing syllables and measuring chapters, has made its way into all the avenues and byways of world literature.

Far away in other lands the book rests in quiet hands, or on wooden shelves and tables. After its cadences were heard by William Butler Yeats, he responded by writing one of his most loved poems, "The Lake Isle of Innisfree." Thus do ripples made by it abroad reach back to the parent pond, and to the village of Concord. These lappings may now come into the newly established Thoreau Lyceum there. This building stands almost beside the railroad tracks where Henry walked the "sleepers" (ties) from the village to Walden Pond, and only a milkweed pod's toss from the site of the "Texas" house on the adjoining lot, where he made pencils while more carefully shaping his own character. In the Lyceum adults and children may now sit and quietly finger pages of the past, or spin cocoon-like dreams of the future.

Language—words which can be put into sentences heavy as iron chains or as light as dandelion-balloons! Distilling nature into thought, Thoreau expressed himself with such clarity that his emphasis now stands out like engraved glass in this age smudged with smog, pollution, and unresolved abstractions of artistic endeavor. Only in man's consciousness of it can time be said to pass, and some books enter time as if it were a castle, and become attendants there. *Walden* is such a book, and in it time is host to the magnitude of a Concord incident—the account of one man's daring odyssey into the far reaches of his identification with nature and with his fellowmen. Here is a word picture almost miraculously successful. Here human aspiration quietly moves while cloud-prints on green meadows seem to remain motionless. Here thought twinkles—but not a picture-star. The anatomy of the story is revealed as coolly as a flower unfolds to show its veined, exquisite center.

To give us anchorage, beliefs, impressions—this would seem to be the office of art amid the nerves of man's awareness held high above the sensation of sinking history. But can a worded thought be as real as a common pebble? Can a word be self-supporting? Can it be something one may eat like a berry? Thoreau wrote as if he regarded the letters of words as living cells, as if the words he needed for his use were as alive as anything, and in the Concord scene, he strung them into sentences strong as ropes and cables. Feeling at home in his own life, and standing in the deepest glades of Concord's historic atmosphere, he was able to find his own identity in words as precisely as he was able to find kinship in nature. They were a luxury he was always able to afford. He was so rich in them, he never once felt impelled to counterfeit a word to portray a thought or feeling.

There he stood beside his pond, perhaps on a "delicious" evening at the close of a satin Sunday, when words, ideas and passages of his journals were gathering and crystallizing for his book. Time, then, must actually have seemed to him to be centered in Concord, and reality must have been as intimate and limpid as the cool water near his feet. So quietly did he stand, the rustle of a leaf, or the fall of an acorn, could have been a reminder that the hour had come, and the way was open to him to put all three—time, reality and *Walden* into the shining crystals of language.

MORE THOUGHTS BY THOREAU

The fate of the Country does not depend on how you vote at the polls—the worst man is as strong as the best at that game; it does not depend on what kind of paper you drop into the ballot-box once a year, but on what kind of man you drop from your chamber into the street every morning.

From Slavery in Massachusetts

Do what you reprove yourself for not doing. Know that you are neither satisfied nor dissatisfied with yourself without reason.

From the JOURNAL, 1850

The pleasures of the intellect are permanent, the pleasures of the heart are transitory.

From the JOURNAL, January 22, 1852

The man of science, who is not seeking for expression but for a fact to be expressed merely, studies nature as a dead language. I pray for such inward experience as will make nature significant.

From the JOURNAL, May 10, 1853

How can we expect a harvest who have not had seed-time of character?

From the JOURNAL, August 7, 1854

CONSERVATIONIST

Henry David Thoreau (1817-1862)
American Naturalist, Philosopher, Writer

Walden and Thoreau's *Journal* reflect his oneness with nature. *Cape Cod* describes his several walking tours of the Cape. Today the National Seashore Park on Cape Cod is a haven for sightseers, hikers, bicyclers, and bathers.

ON EMERSON

Ralph Waldo Emerson (1803-1882)
American Essayist, Philosopher, Poet

"Wherever there is knowledge, wherever there is virtue, wherever there is beauty, he will find a home," wrote Emerson about

Thoreau (quoted in the article "New Bust in the Hall of Fame" which begins this section). What about Emerson himself today?

Hyatt H. Waggoner in *American Poets from the Puritans to the Present* concludes on the last pages of his book:

> Our poets are starting this time where Emerson started almost a century and a half ago, searching personal experience for transcendent values, values that link becoming with Being. They are looking for the light within experience, not beyond it, cultivating modes of apprehension that will permit them to see the sparks within the darkness itself (page 632).
> Poetry is a sustaining force when it is read, not when it is talked about. The knowledge it offers is primarily personal and inward, an increased awareness. Our poets are the Sayers who tell us both who we are and where we are, the Namers who give us the words and images that relate us to the world, the tellers of the news that is not stale tomorrow (page 633).

Let Emerson speak to you himself in his own words from such essays as "Intellect," The American Scholar," "Circles," and "Compensation." His words may express just the idea of comfort or encouragement you now need in your own educational endeavors, or they may stimulate you to do more thinking on your own.

> What is the hardest task in the world? To think. I would put myself in the attitude to look in the eye an abstract truth, and I cannot. I blench and withdraw on this side and on that. . . . It seems as if we needed only the stillness and composed attitude of the library, to seize the thought. But we come in, and are as far from it as at first. Then, in a moment, and unannounced, the truth appears. A certain wandering light appears, and is the distinction, the principle we wanted. But the oracle comes because we had previously laid siege to the shrine. . . . We are all wise. The difference between persons is not in wisdom but in art. . . . Perhaps, if we should meet Shakespeare, we should not be conscious of any steep inferiority; no: but of a great equality— only that he possessed a strange skill of using, of classifying his facts, which we lacked.

In every man's mind, some images, words, and facts remain, without effort on his part to imprint them, which others forget, and afterward these illustrate to him the important laws. All our progress is an unfolding, like the vegetable bud. You have first an instinct, then an opinion, then a knowledge, as a plant has root, bud and fruit. Trust the instinct to the end, though you can render no reason. It is vain to hurry it. By trusting it to the end, it shall ripen into truth, and you shall know why you believe. Each mind has its own method.

What is addressed to us for contemplation does not threaten us, but makes us intellectual beings. The growth of intellect is spontaneous in every step. The mind that grows could not predict the times, the means, the mode of that spontaneity.

The Scholar is that man who must take up unto himself all the ability of the time, all the contributions of the past, all the hopes of the future. He must be a university of knowledge. If there be one lesson more than another which should pierce his ear, it is: The world is nothing, and you know not yet how a globule of sap ascends; in yourself slumbers the whole of Reason; it is for you to know all; it is for you to dare all. . . . This confidence in the unsearched might of man belongs to all motives, by all prophecy, by all preparation, to the American scholar.

The life of a man is a self-evolving circle, which, from a ring imperceptibly small, rushes on all sides outwards to new and longer circles, and that without end. . . . The continual effort to raise himself above himself, to work a pitch above his last height, betrays itself in a man's relations. . . . Literature is a point outside of our hodiernal circle, through which a new one may be described. The use of literature is to afford us a platform whence we may command a view of our present life, a purchase by which we may move it.

And yet the compensations of calamity are made apparent to the understanding, also, after long intervals of time. A fever, a mutilation, a cruel disappointment, a loss of wealth, a loss of friends, seem at the moment unpaid loss, and unpayable. But the sure years reveal the deep remedial force that underlies all facts. The death of a dear friend, wife, brother, lover, which seemed nothing but privation, somewhat later assumes the aspect of a guide or genius; for it commonly operates revolutions in our way of life, terminates an epoch of infancy or of youth which was waiting to be closed, breaks up a wanted occupation, or a household, or style of living, and allows the formation of new ones more friendly to the growth of character. It permits or constrains the formation of new acquaintances, and the reception of new influences that prove of the first importance to the next years; and the man or woman who would have remained a sunny garden flower, with no room for its roots and too much sunshine for its head, by the falling of the walls and the neglect of the garden, is made the banyan of the forest, yielding shade and fruit to wide neighborhoods of men.

ON DICKINSON

A SUMMARY OF THE DISSERTATION
*"Mysticism in the Poetry of Emily Dickinson"**
by Emma J. Phillips

This dissertation undertakes to show that the poetry of Emily Dickinson is best understood as a dramatic modern exploration of the two levels of consciousness which blend to constitute the mystic's view of total Reality. Whether the poetic persona is assuming the role of the deep Self, identified with the Supreme Being, or the finite role of the lonely ego, her underlying consciousness of this doubleness provides the unity that stirs the reader to a glimpse of the infinite perspective. This perspective includes the limitations of the scientist's relative view, and both supports and is supported by the scepticism indispensable to his legitimate mode of attacking his problems. Science supports mysticism by discovering its own limitations through its own method of investigation, and mysticism supports science by providing at the center of Being the security so essential to the success of its contribution to the Creator's evolutionary process in time and space. Thus mysticism is validated by Emily Dickinson's uncompromisingly existential approach to the experience of daily life. Her clear recognition of the inevitable residue of

----

*Dr. Phillips received her Ph.D. from Indiana University in June, 1967. She was a member of the Department of English, at Palm Beach Junior College, Lake Worth, Florida at that time. Used with permission.

scientific uncertainty concerning life's most vital issues, points as unerringly to the Infinite as does the large body of her explicit reference to "the syllableless sea."

To: Dr. Harold C. Manor, President, Palm Beach Junior College*
From: Miss Emma J. Phillips, English Instructor at Palm Beach Junior College
Subject: Report on leave of absence for doctoral study of Emily Dickinson, the effect of this study on subsequent teachings, and the compatibility of such teachings with *America Is People and Ideas* by Mrs. Dorothy Myers Peed.

I had expected my study of Emily Dickinson to benefit my teaching, but was unprepared for the exciting difference—all for the better—that it is making in my work. Aside from the routine consideration that a teacher of writing can more efficiently help his students if he is doing some writing himself, my dissertation has been helpful for two other reasons: (1) it is one of the types of writing that is given a prominent place in freshman composition, that is to say, the research paper, and (2) in its subject matter it has implemented for me a dimension in the philosophy of education that has been sadly neglected in America for many years: the close relationship between the sciences and the humanities, a perception of which is badly needed to support the spiritual values of life. The college years, as is well known, are the ones in which most young people make their most strenuous efforts to formulate a satisfying philosophy of life, and the readings in the freshman anthologies are geared to the students' need in this respect by presenting opposing views on many pressing issues. It is in handling this material that my work on the dissertation has effected a radical change in organization, interpretation, and approach, because basically my dissertation was an in-depth study of the struggle of one person (the poetic genius, Emily Dickinson) to bridge the gap between modern scientific developments and the goal of the humanities: the ability to see life whole. In response, the interest of the students is highly gratifying. This is the most refreshing teaching experience I have had since my initial enthusiasm over college teaching as contrasted with teaching on the high school level.

---

*Used with permission. Dr. Phillips as of June, 1967.

In fairness I must add, however, that this inspiration is not solely due to my work on the dissertation, but also to its very happy combination with my use of Mrs. Dorothy Myers Peed's book *America Is People and Ideas*, a guide to library research "for the Space Age." This book is unique for its revelation of inter-disciplinary relationships and its heartening emphasis on the contribution of science to the spiritual destiny of the human race. Students appear most eager for this evaluation of science in a spiritual context, a context of which my recent study has given me a distinct view for the first time. It is surely of funda-mental importance that the teacher's own philosophy of life be clearly formulated. This insight is implemented ideally by the approach to scientific research presented in Mrs. Peed's book. In this scientific age, the interest of students, with their background of scientific training, is most readily enlisted by scientific topics for investigation such as this book suggests, and they would scarcely be able to appreciate the spiritual values they are seeking if they were presented through any other medium. Following this lead, my courses are being enlivened by daily recourse to current newspapers and periodical literature for which our anthology provides an integrating frame of reference. In short, I have a whole new perspective on my courses. As a final word of appreciation for the leave of absence granted me, I can say that it is the perspective gained through my work on my dissertation that has given me my present phi-losophy for my composition courses and appreciation of the potential contribution of Mrs. Peed's book to that philosophy. My students are now benefiting from it.

PART THREE
ENGLISH MECHANICS

ON WORDS

*THOUGHT PROVOKERS
AND
SENTENCE STRUCTURE STUDY*

The knowledge of words is the gate of scholarship.

WILSON

Words are both better and worse than thoughts; they express them, and add to them; they give them power for good or evil; they start on an endless flight, for instruction and comfort and blessing, or for injury and sorrow and ruin.

TRYON EDWARDS

The finest words in the world are only vain sounds if you cannot comprehend them.

ANATOLE FRANCE

"Sizes" of Thoughts. On the next two pages a flow chart, here called the Thinking Chart, will qualify the meaning of the word *thought* according to the "size" or "complexity" of the implication of thought in each usage. But first—

A Prehistory. Homo sapiens begins to communicate by voice and develops tools for representing thoughts which we call WORDS. See the December, 1976, issue of the *National Geographic* for the report of the three-to-four-million-year-old "Family" of Man discovered by anthropologists in Ethiopia. These are the oldest remains of the genus Homo. Now imagine how this family communicated and developed Grunt language.

The English Language reflects its history. Latin, Greek, German, French, etc., all contributed to the corporate language.

When man developed the need for complex sentences, he had provided himself with the communication tool necessary for scientific, philosophical or technological thinking.

THE THINKING CHART

"SIZE" OF THOUGHTS

WORDS	VOCABULARY	SENTENCES
th	½th+th	<u>th</u>

The NEED to name things, to indicate actions, to qualify them, to show relationships and to join ideas, all leads to the development of "parts of speech," which number eight in English. We label this word-size thought "th" and recognize it as an important tool for communication.

Homo sapiens's NEEDS multiply and with usage develop a vocabulary. A prepositional idea becomes attached to the beginning of a word as a prefix which adds to the thought of the word—th—and is a ½th.
Likewise, word endings called **suffixes** change the use, but not the meaning, of a word.

The unit of thought which requires subject and predicate is the sentence, <u>th</u>, and can be simple, compound, or complex. A compound sentence is two simple sentences joined by a conjunction. A complex sentence is "complicated" because the main idea of the sentence has one or more ideas dependent on the main idea.

th=word	½th=prefix	<u>th</u>=sentence

PARAGRAPH	COMPOSITION	RESEARCH PAPER
TH	TH	TH

Para, Greek prefix (beside)+*graph*, the Greek verb (to write). Paragraph is a large unit of thought containing several sentences on one point. It has a topic sentence which is placed in the paragraph according to the development of the thought in the paragraph. There are several methods for developing a paragraph-size thought unit.

Com, Latin prefix (with)+*posi*, Latin (to place)+tion (noun-forming suffix). Composition is several paragraphs combined to form an even larger thought unit than a paragraph.

A research paper is usually longer than a composition and is based on information acquired in the library, by questionnaire survey, or by other means. It is based on a proposition, or thesis. A thesis statement in the form of a complex sentence may also be a brief outline of the thesis.

TH=paragraph   TH=composition   TH=research paper

ENGLISH, THE BORROWED LANGUAGE, AND THE DICTIONARY

From Germanic tribesmen in northern Europe to Shakespeare's writings is a fifteen-hundred-year accounting of conquest and struggle for identity reflected in the English language. Early Modern English is a true amalgamation—a uniting, mixing, combining, and consolidation. A complete study of the vocabulary, grammar, and pronunciation of this borrowed language is suggested. Begin with these ideas.

Think of the British Isles as the battleground of both the peoples who conquered and settled, and the languages which contributed to English. Note the locations and the dates in the sketch below.

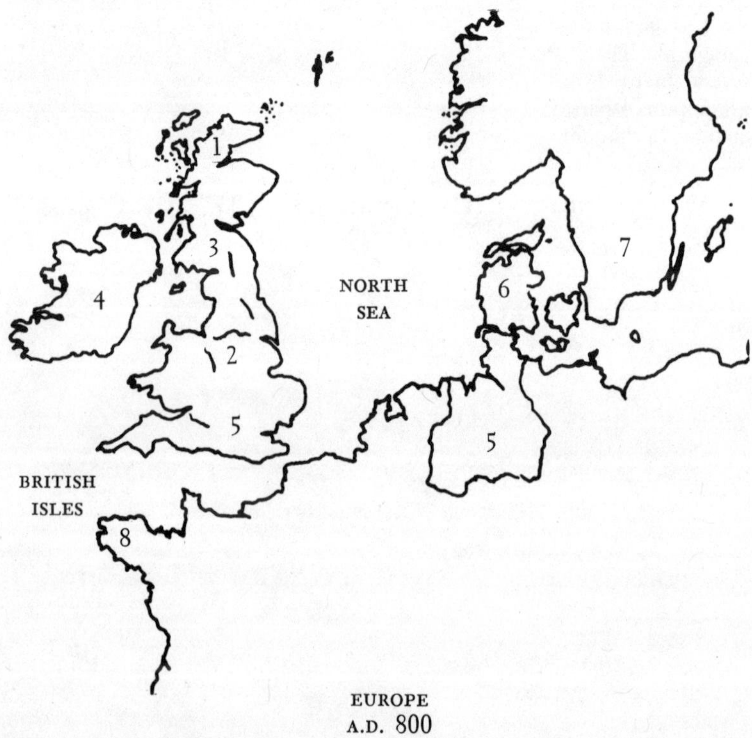

1 Picts
2 Britons
3 Scots
4 Celts (Roman Conquest, A.D. 43)*
5 Anglo Saxons, fifth century
6 Jutes (Roman Church, Latin)
7 Danes (Vikings), ninth century
8 French, William the Conqueror, 1066 (military and political)
   Anglo-Saxon becomes a language with the accent of the London
   area, c. 1200

Indo European (IE) is the hypothetical language reconstructed by modern linguists from which the Germanic family of languages—among many others—is believed to have descended. English belongs to this Germanic family which includes German, Dutch, Flemish, Danish, Norwegian, Icelandic, and Swedish. The Germans were pagans until the Romans brought Christianity to them together with Latin and the Roman alphabet.

A classification of the periods of the English Language and their time spans are:

Old English (OE)	450-1050
Middle English (ME)	1050-1475
Early Modern English (EMnE)	1475-1700
Late Modern English (LMnE)	1700-

KNOWLEDGE OF LATIN VITAL
TO UNDERSTANDING ENGLISH†

by Sydney J. Harris

A high school student in West Virginia has written to ask me if I think he should continue with his Latin studies. "Has Latin done you any good?" he inquires, "and is it useful in your work?"

The answer is yes to both these questions. Nobody can speak, write, or understand English properly unless he has some rudimentary knowledge of Latin. For English is a hybrid language—

---

*Read "Who Really Discovered America?" by Thomas Fleming in the *Reader's Digest* for February, 1977.

†Reprinted by permission of Sydney J. Harris and Field Newspaper Syndicate.

fewer than half our words are native, and the rest borrowed from foreign tongues, mostly Latin.

In no other language, for instance, do we find so many native nouns taking Latin adjectives. The adjective for "mouth" is not "mouthy" but "oral" which is straight from the Latin.

Likewise, "nose" gives us "nasal," "eye" gives us "ocular," "mind" gives us "mental," "son" gives us "filial," "house" gives us "domestic," "sun" and "moon" gives us "solar" and "lunar." There are hundreds of similar cases.

We don't even have native English adjectives for the four seasons: fall is "autumnal," winter is "hibernal," spring is "vernal," and summer is "estival." The first words a child learns, "mama" and "daddy," take Latin adjectives—"maternal" and "paternal."

English is primarily a "loan language." If you want to know how much, read any of the books by Otto Jesperson, the great Danish philologist, and you may be surprised at the enormous debt we owe not only to Latin and Greek but also to the Scandinavian languages, to French, and even to the Germanic influences upon Old English.

A foreigner learning English would find it insuperably difficult if he did not have a solid base in Latin.

This explains why educated foreigners are able to pick up our tongue so rapidly, and why some uneducated foreigners can live here thirty years without really grasping the language.

As an important parenthesis, I found my own Latin (shaky as it is) of great use while traveling through Europe. I was able to get along handily in Italian after only six weeks of living in Florence, and my French is at least passable, using the glue of Latin to stick together French and English words.

Studying the classic languages is neither a waste of time nor a form of intellectual snobbishness; it is, rather, the quickest and most permanent way to master one's own tongue and to become a genuine citizen in the community of man, past and present.

The following jingle that appears in Estelle B. Hunter's *A New Self-Help Course in Practical English and Effective Speech, Lesson One* (Chicago: The Better-Speech Institute of America, 1936) will become a very useful set of rules when you study grammar. Let the rhythm of the lines help you memorize it.

THE EIGHT PARTS OF SPEECH

All names of persons, places, things,
Are NOUNS, as Caesar, Rome, and kings.

PRONOUNS are used in place of nouns:
I think; she sings; they work; he frowns.

When the kind you wish to state,
Use an ADJECTIVE, as great.

But if of manner you would tell,
Use ADVERBS, such as slowly, well.
To find an adverb, this test try:
Ask, "How?" or "When?" or "Where?" or "Why?"

PREPOSITIONS show relation,
As with respect, or in our nation.

CONJUNCTIONS, as their name implies,
Are joining words; they are the ties
That bind together day and night,
Calm but cold, dull or bright.

Next we have the VERBS, which tell
Of action, being and state as well.
To work, succeed, achieve, and curb—
Each one of these is called a VERB.

The INTERJECTIONS show surprise,
As Oh! Alas! Ah me! How wise!
Thus briefly does this jingle state
The PARTS OF SPEECH, which total eight.

THE DICTIONARY

Page 9 lists the tools necessary for a Self-Help Course in Basics. A *good* dictionary is listed first for what are now obvious reasons. A *good* dictionary has been specified so that you will have at your fingertips the wealth of information about word history, spelling, usage, and definitions, which the serious student of language and written communication must have. Examine your own dictionary in the following manner (if you have more than one dictionary, do a comparative study, for dictionaries reflect different schools of thought regarding linguistics):

- Find the page headed Symbols and Language Abbreviations, or words to that effect, and become acquainted with the abbreviations you will probably find in your word study. Plan to refer to this page regularly.

- Glance through the Table of Contents—you may be amazed at the wealth of information, other than word study, that your dictionary provides. By contrast, an 1849 Noah Webster (revised edition) dictionary includes an Addenda with "A Classical Pronunciation of Greek, Latin, and Scriptural Proper Names"; the derivation of words is very sparse, indicating the need for study of linguistics and etymology, which is a branch of linguistics dealing with the origin and development of words.

- Study the following signs and abbreviations, together with examples of etymology as they appear in brackets, [ ], in dictionaries, and note how the history of English has helped you understand the derivations of words. Purposely, words have been selected which have an IE base and/or illustrate a prefix or suffix on the root word.

Signs and Abbreviations in Dictionary Definitions

An asterisk (*) indicates that the definition given is a hypothetical one, arrived at by linguistics scholars.

akin=like	MFr=Middle French
<=comes from	G=German
pp=past participle of the verb	L=Latin
com-=prefix	Gmc=Germanic
-ary=suffix	ME=Middle English
n=noun	Gr=Greek
v=verb	ML=Middle Latin
	AS=Anglo-Saxon
	IE=Indo-European

Examples of Derivations:
1. *colloquium*, n [L *colloquium*, conversation < *com-*, together
   + *loqui*, to speak-]
2. *dictionary*, n [ML, *dictionarium*; L, *dictio*; a speaking < pp
   of *dicere*, to say; IE *deik-*, to point out, show as also in G
   zeigen, to show, AS, *teon*, to accuse + -ary, suffix meaning
   relating to . . .]
3. *mother*, n [ME, *moder*; AS, *moder*; akin to G, *mutter*; IE,
   mater, mother . . .]
4. *father*, n [ME, *fader*; AS *faeder*; common Gmc; akin to G,
   vater; IE, *pater*, whence also L *pater*, Gr, *pater* . . .]
5. *family*, n [L. *familia*, servants in a household, *famulus*, servant;
   IE, *dhe-mo*; house . . .]

NOTICE that the derivation of colloquium gives *com* rather
than *col* as the prefix. Look up *com* as prefix and you will understand why the consonant is changed; this same change of prefix
form is true of many prefixes for the same reason, notably *in*
which has two families of variations according to whether *in* is a
preposition or a negative in meaning. Have you observed that
prefixes are listed in the dictionary with a dash (—) after the prefix and then the meaning? In the same manner, suffixes are listed
with a dash before the suffix followed by an indication of the
part of speech that the suffix forms on the root word.

TURN the pages of your dictionary and examine words at
random. Note that scientists, scholars, poets, and ordinary citizens
have had, and are having, a part in changing the language and
in adding to the vocabulary. Review the Thought Provokers on
language, page 31.

FORM the habit of turning regularly to the Word Power section of the *Reader's Digest* to prove to yourself how this study
of words, and perhaps a little knowledge of Latin, helps you build
Word Power. Look at the answer page first until you recognize
the prefix-root-suffix parts of words. Note how Latin often gives
you the clue to the correct answer.

INCREASE your vocabulary by finding a self-help, vocabulary-
building book which is based on *roots, prefixes,* and *suffixes;* or

work out a study program for yourself by looking up every prefix you can think of in your dictionary. Here are a few to begin with: *in-, ex-, inter-, re-, trans-, contra-, mis-, anti-, manu-, ab-, ad-, per-.* Do the same for suffixes beginning with: *-ant, -ness, -ive, -ing, -ful, -hood, -or, -ed.*

FIND *roots* by looking up the word "factory." You may be referred to factor for the derivation—Latin *facere,* to make. Now find other words on the same pages which come from the same root. Attach a prefix like *manu-* and see what you have—*manufacture.* Study this word and others you may produce by adding a prefix or suffix to the root.

LOOK up "dictionary." Has the derivation given in this section been combined from *diction* and *ary?* Add a prefix like *contra-* and you have *contradiction.* Study the prefix, root, and suffix and then find other words in the *diction* family.

We should not leave this section without considering other forms of language. They would be called symbolic language, and you may be familiar with many of them.

    Music
    Therbligs, in industrial engineering
    Signal flags
    Buoys
    Morse Code
    Hand signals, in sports
    Hand signals, by which the deaf communicate
    Weather signs
    Chemistry and physics symbols
    Traffic signs

You continue the list. Could it be that there is a kind of structure and/or grammar in these symbolic languages?

ON ORDER

*THOUGHT PROVOKERS
AND
SENTENCE STRUCTURE STUDY*

Order is heaven's first law.

POPE

Order is the sanity of the mind, the health of the body, the peace of the city, the security of the state. As the beams to a house, as the bones to the body, so is order in all things.

SOUTHEY

We do not keep the outward form of order where there is deep disorder in the mind.

SHAKESPEARE

Order means light and peace, inward liberty and free command over one's self; order is power.

AMIEL

Good order is the foundation of all good things.

BURKE

So, let us develop order in our thoughts so there will be grammatical order in our writing.

Hence the pages which follow.

Early in the directions for Your Own Writings which appear throughout this book, the suggestion was made to turn to the section on Englsh mechanics for review. Some readers may have found it advisable to study the section carefully before returning to the reading and paragraph writing suggestions.

At whatever point you use the following pages, certain study helps throughout this book and tools should be at hand.

Reread the quotations on ORDER as the Thought Provokers for this section. They have been selected with care, for *grammar assists the ordering of the mind.*

Review:

Page 128: the map of the British Isles and Europe A.D. 800, showing English as a borrowed language.
Page 182: sentences in seven different languages to show that grammar varies with the language.
Page xi: the Preface, for the reference to parsing.
Page 126: The Thinking Chart, especially the first half.
Page 35: A Conversation About Language.

Have at Hand:

Your *good* dictionary which is more valuable than you now realize. Find the section on The English Language which is usually in the Introduction. Use your dictionary constantly to look up grammar terms or any other words you do not understand.
An English handbook for more detailed information on style and form in writing.

NOUNS
Latin nomen (name, noun)

If you have memorized the jingle "Eight Parts of Speech," page 131, you may already have recognized that as a definition of a noun, the first couplet is incomplete. To prove this for yourself, check off the nouns in the previous Thought Provokers on Order. Use the dictionary definition for nouns as words that "name some person, *thing, quality,* etc."

You will find that this definition comes nearer to helping you recognize why such words as order, sanity, health, peace, security, form, disorder, liberty, command, power (you find others) are nouns.

With this enlarged definition in mind, let us find out how much we should know about nouns, and let us use that old-fashioned process of parsing to do so. When you parse a word in a sentence, you tell all you know about the form, the part of speech, and the function of the word in the sentence: kind, gender, number, person, case, use.

KINDS

Proper: names of particular people, places, things—always written with a capital.

Common: one of a group or class, such as book, boy, bench.

Collective: a group or collection, as orchestra, family. Collective nouns may be thought of in the singular or plural; the verb being in the singular or plural designates singular or plural intent. For example:

The family are all home today. (Each family member is considered separately, so the verb is plural.)

The orchestra plays that selection with great enthusiasm. (The orchestra is functioning as a group, hence the singular verb.)

Abstract: expresses a quality apart from the material—not concrete.

GENDER

Gender may be masculine, feminine, or neuter. In the "borrowing" process of the development of English, nouns lost their designation of gender. Thus the English articles, *the*, *a*, *an*, do not have to agree with the noun in gender as is true in many foreign languages. Turn to the foreign language sentences, page 182, and note *una persona* or *la personne*, *la grammaire* or *la grammatica*. They are all feminine in form in their languages, and so are indicated by the feminine *la* rather than the masculine article. In English we generally consider nouns to be neuter.

NUMBER

The singular or plural of nouns present spelling problems. Most nouns add *s* to form the plural:

pencil, pencils   book, books

But if, in forming the plural, the word acquires another syllable, to represent that sound add *es*.

box, boxes   church, churches

Words like man-men and child-children change the form considerably; you know many more examples.

The final *y* or *ey* on a noun also determines the plural spelling.

lady, ladies—but pulley, pulleys

When you change the *y* to *ie* and add the *s*, as in ladies, you have two vowels together. But if you were to do the same for pulley, you would have three vowels in a row, and English does not like that.

Forming the plural of proper nouns is a problem. Remember, if a noun ends in *s*, to make it plural, you add *es*:

Hutchins, Hutchinses

If the noun does not end in *s* you add only the *s*.

Hortman, Hortmans

Forming the possessive of proper nouns is another problem which will be discussed in the paragraphs on Case and Use.

PERSON

First, second, and third persons are more characteristic of pronouns than of nouns. This will be evident in the section on pronouns. But if we consider person for nouns, they would be third person, singular or plural in number. The pronouns that would refer to them would be *it* for the singular and *they, them, those,* etc., for the plural.

CASE

Case is a leftover from the "borrowed" languages which had many different cases; English now recognizes the nominative, possessive, and objective cases. That which determines the case of the noun or pronoun in the sentence structure is the use.

Observe the Latin sentence on page 182 for a use of the objective case. (In Latin this is called the accusative case.) The *am* endings of the nouns *grammaticam* and *linguam* indicate that these are objects of the respective verbs (in English, *knows and learn*). Note, also that *barbaram*, which is an adjective, is in the same case as the noun it modifies. This is a Latin grammar rule. In English grammar, only in pronouns are we aware of the nominative or objective case.

The *possessive case*, however, is obvious because of the spelling which often presents problems. You indicate the possessive of nouns be adding an 's when it is singular:

> child—child's
> woman—woman's
> Charles—Charles's
> actress—actress's

But if the noun is plural and, therefore, ends in s or es you add only the apostrophe (').

> actresses—actresses'
> nurses—nurses'
> Hutchinses—Hutchinses'

A general rule is to write the word as you want it in the singular or plural. Then consider how to make the word possessive. If it would make another syllable by adding both the apostrophe and *s* to form the plural possessive, then add only the apostrophe. Otherwise add both the apostrophe and *s*. Examples:

Nominative *Singular*	*Possessive* *Singular*	*Possessive* *Plural*
niece	niece's	nieces'
Hortman	Hortman's	Hortmans'
Hutchins	Hutchins's	Hutchinses'

USE

Nouns are used in the *nominative case*:

1. as the subject (S) of the verb or as the predicate nominative (PN):

S   PN
Order is heaven's law.

2. in direct address:

Readers, you can add other examples.

Nouns are used in the *objective case*:

1. as the direct object (DO) of a verb (V) or preposition (OP):

V   DO OP
We keep the outward form of order . . .

2. as the indirect object (IO) of a verb:

IO
Reading gives the student satisfaction.

(Note that the above sentence uses the *ing* form of the verb *to read* to form the gerund, *reading,* which is a verbal noun. It is here used as the subject of the sentence. A verbal noun is called a gerund.)

Nouns are used in the *possessive case*:

1. as possessive adjectives (PosA):

Pos A

Order is heaven's first law.

2. as subject of a gerund (ger):

S   ger

The student's reading gave him satisfaction.

(Noun clauses will be examined in the section on sentence structure.)

PRONOUNS

Latin pro (for) nomen (noun, name)

As the Latin for pronoun implies, a pronoun is a word which substitutes for a noun, thus adding convenience to the language.

Though you may think of personal pronouns as the only kind of pronoun to study, there actually are several kinds of pronouns to be considered. The list would read: Personal, Relative, Indefinite, Interrogative, Demonstrative, Reciprocal, Intensive, and Reflexive.

PERSONAL PRONOUNS

Personal pronouns change form according to the person, number, and sex of the noun to which the pronoun refers. The person of a pronoun is designated as 1st, 2nd, 3rd. They are defined as:

the person speaking—1st person
the person spoken to—2nd person
the person spoken of—3rd person

The number of the pronoun is singular or plural and the sex is masculine, feminine, or neuter. The personal pronouns are:

	Singular	Plural
1st	I	we
2nd	you	you
3rd	he, she, it	they

Your selection of the correct pronoun in your speech or writing requires more consideration than just the person, number, or sex of the referent, the noun to which the pronoun refers. The USE of the pronoun in the sentence is very important—so important, in fact, that the selection you make indicates your understanding of grammar and/or your caring to speak and write correct English. This same telltale indication of your knowledge of English sentence structure is shown in the verbs you use—especially the verb forms you use with the third-person pronouns.

Before reading on, review page 139 on the CASE and USE of nouns.

To summarize, modern English has no change of ending to denote case of nouns as do the parent languages. But the spelling of pronouns in English is so varied in accordance with the use of the pronoun in the sentence, that they seem to be different words. So, you must be sure that you understand the use of the pronoun in the sentence to make the proper selection of pronoun form.

The following Chart of Personal Pronouns gives you the form for the various persons, number, and uses in the sentence. Study it and refer to it until the forms become automatic for you to use.

CHART OF PERSONAL PRONOUNS

Case:	Nominative	Objective	Possessive	
Use:	Subject of verb or predicate nominative	Object of verb (direct, or indirect) or object of preposition	Pronoun	Adjective
	Person			
Singular	1st I	me	mine	my
	2nd you	you	yours	your
	3rd he, she, it	him, her, it	his, hers, its	his, hers, its
Plural	1st we	us	ours	our
	2nd you	you	yours	your
	3rd they	them	theirs	their

Studying the chart, we see that pronouns in the *nominative case* may be *predicate nominatives* as well as *subjects* in the sentence. This means that the noun or pronoun in the predicate is interchangeable with the subject, or nominative. Example:

I am John.   I am <u>he</u>.
I am the owner.   The owner is <u>I</u>.
We must be good citizens.   It is <u>we</u> who must be good citizens.

The underlined words may appear and sound strange to you. The subject of each sentence is in the nominative case and the pronoun following each verb refers to the subject. Both must, therefore, be nominative, and the pronoun in the predicate is considered a predicate nominative. The choice of verb is important with this pronoun form. It is called an intransitive, or linking, verb. More in another section.

The *objective case* can be understood by examining the Latin word from which it is taken. *Objectivus* means "something thrown in the way," from Latin *ob* (to, toward) + *jacere* (to throw). The object in a sentence receives the action of the verb—receives the action of the throwing—and so the pronoun in the examples below is in the objective case. In English we do not usually refer to case so the word could be omitted from the chart. Examples:

Reading educates *us* (direct object).
Understanding gives *us* courage (indirect object).
Please give the message *to us* immediately (object of preposition).

Note: You will not be using good grammar if you use a pronoun in the OBJECTIVE column as the subject of the sentence. You will not be using good grammar if you use a pronoun in the NOMINATIVE column as the object of a verb or preposition.

Why would the following be incorrect?

John and me will be there.
He gave Mary and I permission.

Do not substitute "myself" (reflexive pronoun) for the pronoun subject in a sentence. (See page 146 for the use of reflexive pronouns.)

The word *possessive* comes from the Latin word *possidere* (to possess). By their very nature possessives modify. To quote the dictionary, "they limit or restrict that which is possessed." They often act like adjectives, and when pronouns do this they are considered possessive adjectives. Hence, the two columns in the chart. Examples:

> The book is *mine* (possessive pronoun).
> This is *my* book (possessive adjective).

Note the spelling of *its* as the possessive pronoun and/or adjective. The possessive form of the pronoun is never spelled "it's," even though the use of an apostrophe seems to be correct. Think of this as a possible explanation for this spelling: "He's" may have been the original spelling and through carelessness in writing the "he's" could have come to look like "his." After all, the feminine is spelled *hers* with no apostrophe. There are such words as "it's" and "he's." They are contractions for "it is" and "he is," respectively.

OTHER PRONOUN FORMS

Nominative	Objective	Possessive
	Relative	
who	whom	whose
that	that	
which	which	
	Indefinite	
one	one	one's
no one	no one	no one's
someone	someone	someone's
everyone	everyone	everyone's
either	either	either's
neither	neither	neither's
each	each	

Interrogative

who?	whom?	whose?
which?	which?	
what?		

Demonstrative

this	this
that	that
these	these
those	those

Reciprocal

each other	each other	each other's
one another	one another	one another's

Intensive or Reflexive

myself	ourselves
yourself	yourselves
himself	themselves

Several of the following sentences are from Thought Provokers (pages as indicated). Determine antecedents from context of quotations.

Relative:

No man has lived *who* has not known . . . ; or *who* . . . .
  Page 99
We have the newspaper *which* does its best. . . . Page 87
The person *whom* the caller wanted to see was not at home.
  (Why use *whom* in this sentence?)

(Note that the relative pronoun *who* refers to people, *which* to things, and *that* to either, though usually things.)

Indefinite:

One can never be sure about such things.
To *each* his own.

(Can you think of an explanation for there *not* being indefinite pronouns in the kind of quotations used in these pages?)

Interrogative:

> What hath God wrought?
> Who goes there?

(See the discussion on prepositions for uses of the journalists'
W's.)

Reflexive:

Accustom *yourself* to thinking. . . . Page 73
. . . give an account of *itself*. . . . Page 87
. . . a deeper understanding of *ourselves*. . . . Page 99

Look up "demonstrative," "reciprocal," and "intensive" pronouns in your dictionary. The definition marked "grammar" will
give you an idea of the use of each of these. Make up your own
examples.

Demonstrative:

Reciprocal:

Intensive:

VERBS
Latin verbum (word)

The word *verb* comes directly from Latin and means word.
It is often the most important word (idea) in the sentence so
care must be taken in selecting the correct form of this word—
this verb.

To select the correct form of the verb, you must know, first,
the number and person of the subject of the verb; second, the
time of the verb idea (present, past, future, etc.); finally, the
kind of verb you are using (transitive or intransitive).

The "Eight Parts of Speech" jingle says that the verbs "tell
of action, being, and state" and gives this example: "to work,
succeed, achieve and curb." These verbs give the rhyme and

rhythm that is neccessary in the jingle. But they are not the best examples of verbs for our discussion here, so we will use, as examples for study, *to be*, *to do*, and *to have* representing existence, action, and possession verbs.

To be is the existence verb, also called the linking verb.

    God *is*.   He *is*.   (existence verb)
    God *is* Love.   God *is* good.   (linking verb)

To do is here used to represent the doing or action verb. Most English verbs are in this group.

    He *does* good deeds wherever he goes.   (action verb)
    They *wrote* letters of inquiry.   (action verb)

To *have* represents verbs of possession.

    He *has* an understanding of the situation.   (possession verb)
    The engineer *owns* a Mazda.   (possession verb)

In the context of "A Conversation About Language," page 35, we can now examine the sentences above and add others to illustrate man's first sentence-speech patterns. To begin with, we can assume that prehistoric man gave simple commands. These would have been verbs with the subject understood. Today this kind of sentence appears as traffic signs such as, *Yield* or *Stop*. The *you* is understood. Reference to the Chart of Personal Pronouns, especially to the headings of the three columns, will help you understand the letters on the simple diagrams which follow. Remember the subject (noun or pronoun) is indicated by a broken line (- - - -) and the predicate (simple verb) by a solid line (__________).

Sᴇɴᴛᴇɴᴄᴇ Sᴛʀᴜᴄᴛᴜʀᴇ

    - - - - - - - - __________ God is. (existence verb)

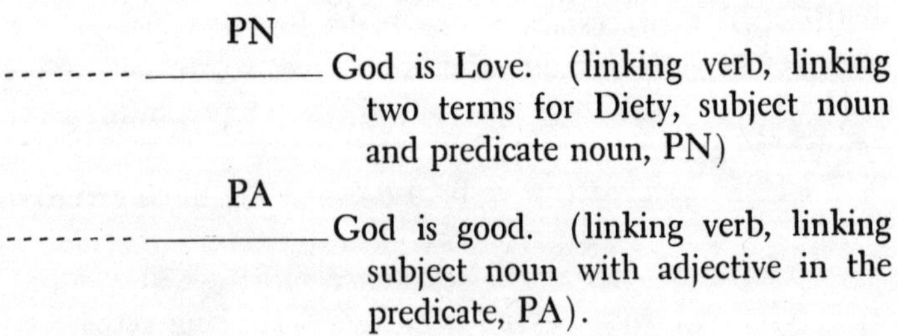

There are two other verbs which express the idea of linking (also called an intransitive verb). They are *to seem* and *to become*. The sentence structure would be the same as above.

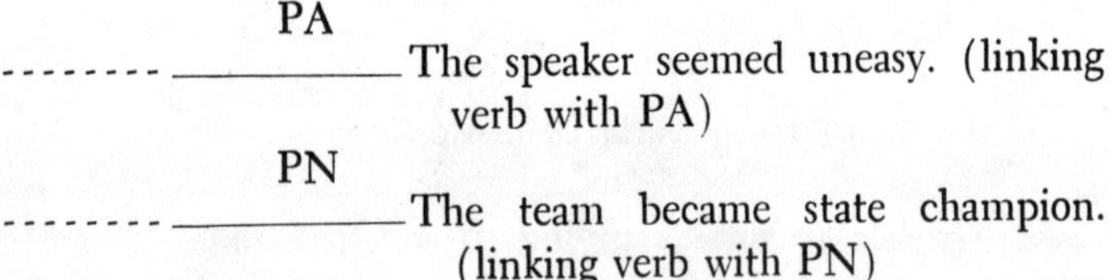

The sentence structure for sentences containing action verbs, represented by *to do*, and the possession verbs represented by *to have*, appear to be the same; but they introduce an entirely different kind of verb—the transitive verb, a verb of action or possession which requires an object to complete the thought.

Before we study further, remind yourself of the derivation of the word *objective* as given in the section on pronouns—*ob* (to or toward) + *jacere* (to throw or to receive the throwing). Objective, therefore, implies that some action is "thrown toward" the word which is the object and that this "throwing" must have significance in the verb. This must refer to a transitive verb, for transitive comes from *trans* (across) + *it* (from *ire*, to go) + *ive* (adjective suffix).

A transitive verb is a verb of *action*, of *doing*, of *having* and sends its meaning across to the noun or pronoun in the predicate of the sentence. This word in the predicate thus becomes the direct object (DO) of the verb. Examples:

<table>
<tr><td align="center">DO
- - - - - - - - - ________</td><td>He does good deeds. (doing verb)</td></tr>
<tr><td align="center">DO
- - - - - - - - ________</td><td>They wrote letters. (action verb)</td></tr>
<tr><td align="center">DO
- - - - - - - - ________</td><td>He has an understanding. (having verb)</td></tr>
<tr><td align="center">DO
- - - - - - - - ________</td><td>The engineer owns a Mazda. (having verb)</td></tr>
</table>

To *work, succeed, achieve,* and *curb* are the verbs in the jingle used to illustrate verbs. If you look these verbs up in the dictionary and study the entire definitions, you will discover that three of these verbs can be used as either transitive or intransitive verbs. *Intransitive* is the negative idea, for the prefix *in* can mean *not* from the Latin. Thus intransitive verbs do not take objects but they often do have predicate nouns (PN) or predicate adjectives (PA) to complete the thought, as observed in the first sentences studied in this section.

When a verb may be either *transitive* or *intransitive,* the function of the verb depends on the defintion of the verb which is applicable to the particular sentence.

<table>
<tr><td align="center">DO
- - - - - - - - ________</td><td>He worked the math problem for us.
She worked miracles. (both verbs are transitive)</td></tr>
<tr><td align="center">DO
- - - - - - - - ________</td><td>His plans worked well.
The cover worked loose. (both verbs are intransitive)</td></tr>
</table>

Transitive verbs may have both a direct and an indirect object. IO is the sign for indirect object. *Note:* the preposition *to* is never used with the indirect object. When it is used, the grammar is a prepositional phrase rather than an indirect object.

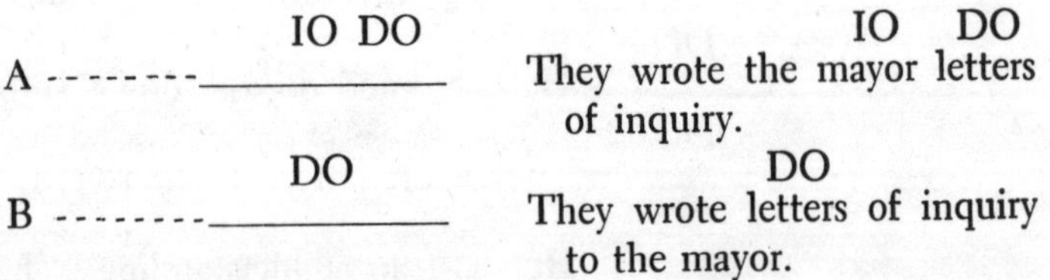

In the non-verbal style of diagraming, a complete diagram of these last two sentences would include parentheses ( ) to represent the phrase. The diagrams, then, would look like this.

There is now only one diagram element which was included in "A Conversation About Language" but not illustrated above. That element is the clause (- - - _______). Because the clause has the same characteristics as a simple sentence, it is not necessary to include the diagram and grammar discussion at this point.

The purpose of this discussion of verbs is to review all possible characteristics of verbs. What has been said was necessary to see a verb functioning in a sentence. What will now be examined are characteristics of verbs themselves.

CONJUGATIONS

We now turn to the forms of verbs, with regard to person and number, tense, and whether the verb is regular or irregular. The word *conjugation* is derived from con (with) + *jugare* (to join) + *tion* (a suffix). From this derivation we see that a conjugation is a joining-together of all the tenses of the verb, and of all the forms for each tense. In other words, there being three persons, 1st, 2nd, 3rd, in the singular and three in the plural for each tense, and there being six simple tenses in a conjugation, there would be, therefore, thirty-six verb and pronoun forms in a conjugation. The six tenses are: present, past, future, present perfect, past perfect, and future perfect.

The three principal parts of a verb are the forms from which all tenses are derived. So, if you know the principal parts, and know the tenses which come from each part, you can put together an entire conjugation of a verb.

We shall do this for two verbs—one a regular verb and one an irregular verb.

In English the regular verb ends in *ed* in the past tense and *ed* in the past participle. Let us use *to grasp* as the regular verb. For the *Principal parts* and the *tenses* from each, we would then have:

(to) grasp	*grasped*	*grasped*
present	past	present perfect
future		past perfect
		future perfect

THE CONJUGATION OF *to grasp*, A REGULAR VERB

Infinitive: to grasp
Present Participle: grasping
Principal Parts: grasp   grasped   grasped

Present Tense	*Present Perfect*
Singular	*Singular*
I grasp	I have grasped
you grasp	you have grasped
he, she, it grasps	he, she, it *has* grasped
Plural	*Plural*
we grasp	we have grasped
you grasp	you have grasped
they grasp	they have grasped
Past Tense	*Past Perfect*
Singular	*Singular*
I grasped	I had grasped
you grasped	you had grasped
he, she, it grasped	he, she, it had grasped

Plural	*Plural*
we grasped	we had grasped
you grasped	you had grasped
they grasped	they had grasped
Future Tense	*Future Perfect*
Singular	*Singular*
I shall grasp	I shall have grasped
you will grasp	you will have grasped
he, she, it will grasp	he, she, it will have grasped
Plural	*Plural*
we shall grasp	we shall have grasped
you will grasp	you will have grasped
they will grasp	they will have grasped

A SYNOPSIS OF *to grasp*, A REGULAR VERB

You can understand what a synopsis is from the derivation of the word synopsis: *syn* (together) + *opsis* (a sight). Therefore a synopsis would be one form from each tense of the verb, that form being the same person and number for each tense.

A synopsis of *to grasp* in the 2nd person singular:

> Present: you grasp
> Past: you grasped
> Future: you will grasp
> Present Perfect: you have grasped
> Past Perfect: you had grasped
> Future Perfect: you will have grasped

Note that we could have formed the synopsis from the principal parts of the verb and the conjugation from the synopsis. If you do not know the principal parts of the verb, you can always find them in the dictionary. In the conjugation, note the *s* in the third singular present and present perfect tenses. This is where a wrong verb form is often spoken. The same is true in the third person of the present perfect tense. Note, also, that the form of the helping verb in the future tense, for the *first person*, both singular and plural, is always *shall* in the future. If you use *will* instead of *shall* in this form, you are making a *promise*. Just the opposite is true for the second and third persons, singular and plural—if you change from *will* to *shall* in these persons, you are then making a promise.

Irregular verb conjugations are more difficult, and so more important for you to know how to determine the forms. For these verbs you may be well advised to check the dictionary for the principal parts. The procedure for doing a conjugation or a synopsis is the same for an irregular as for a regular verb. You should be familiar with *to be*; therefore, it will be used to illustrate an irregular verb.

THE CONJUGATION OF *to be*, AN IRREGULAR VERB

Infinitive: to be
Present Participle: being
Principal Parts:　am　　was　　been

Present Tense

　Singular
I am
you are
he, she, it is

　Plural
we are
you are
they are

Past Tense

　Singular
I was
you were
he, she, it was

　Plural
we were
you were
they were

Future Tense

　Singular
I shall be
you will be
he, she, it will be

Present Perfect Tense

　Singular
I have been
you have been
he, she, it has been

　Plural
we have been
you have been
they have been

Past Perfect Tense

　Singular
I had been
you had been
he, she, it had been

　Plural
we had been
you had been
they had been

Future Perfect Tense

　Singular
I shall have been
you will have been
he, she, it will have been

Future Tense	*Future Perfect Tense*
Plural	*Plural*
we shall be	we shall have been
you will be	you will have been
they will be	they will have been

If you know the principal parts of a verb, you can determine the correct form for any tense your sentences require. Here are the principal parts of more irregular verbs:

Present	Past	Perfect
go	went	gone
come	came	come
think	thought	thought
do	did	done
speak	spoke	spoken
have	had	had
drive	drove	driven
write	wrote	written
see	saw	seen
bite	bit	bitten
take	took	taken
swim	swam	swum
run	ran	run

Note: Careful observation of these columns will give you another opportunity to check on your grammatical errors. All verb forms in the third column (*Perfect*) must be preceded by the auxiliary, or helping, verb *have*—or one of its forms: *has, had,* or *shall have.* If you use the contraction *'ve* before the main verb as in "I've written," you must also select the form for the perfect tense. Thus, it would be poor grammar to say "He done it" or "He seen it" for "He did it" or "He saw it."

Sometimes it is necessary to determine whether the verb you are using is transitive or intransitive in a particular sentence. Three verbs which must be so determined are: to sit, to set; to lie, to lay; to rise, to raise. If you "stretch the meaning" of to *place* and to *recline*, and if you apply these substitute verbs to the irregular verbs we are studying, you will have little trouble understanding which of each pair of verbs to use in specific sentences, even though the correct verb may sound strange to you at first. If you note that *to place* is *transitive* and *to recline* is *intransitive* you will have additional help in selecting the correct forms in your speech and writing.

TRANSITIVE AND INTRANSITIVE IRREGULAR VERBS

Infinitive	Principal Parts	Meaning	Use
to lie	lie lay lain	to recline	intransitive
to lay	lay laid laid	to place	transitive
to rise	rise rose risen	to "recline"	intransitive
to raise	raise raised raised	to "place"	transitive
to sit	sit sat sat	to recline	intransitive
to set	set set set	to place	transitive

Examples:

The dog *lay* beside the master all day. (intransitive, past)
The master *laid* the food dish on the floor. (transitive, past)

The sun *rises* at a different time each day. (intransitive, present)
He *raises* the flag at sunrise daily. (transitive, present)

He will *sit* beside the speaker. (intransitive, future)
He will *set* the water glass on the podium. (transitive, future)

UDERSTANDING SEQUENCE OF TENSES

The proper use of tenses, called the sequence of tenses, depends on a careful analysis of the exact thought you want to express, and on an analysis of the tenses to be used. The correct sequence of tenses requires an understanding of the relationship of present and present perfect, past and past perfect, and future and future perfect. Note that common usage of the future tense often pairs the future with the present rather than the future perfect, perhaps because of the very awkward verb phrase which the future perfect of a verb forms.

A graphic representation of *sequence of tenses* may be gained in the following description of a freshman English class presentation. The chalk board at the front of the lecture room where I taught was in two sections, and the division between the two was both noticeable and in the middle of the front wall. Standing in front of this division, I labeled this area *present tense*. All the chalk board to the left of the students represented some form of the *past tenses*; that to the right represented the *future tenses*.

To complete the three simple tenses, a horizontal block marked "Past" was made in the center of the left board, and one marked "Future" in the center of the right board.

A horizontal line with arrow to "Present" was marked "Present Perfect" (action perfected, or completed, before the present), while one to "Past" was marked "Past Perfect" to indicate that the action had been completed before the action of the past-tense verb.

On the future tense side, the line and arrow to "Future" was marked "Future Perfect" representing action performed or completed before the time of the action of the main verb in the future tense.

SEQUENCE OF TENSES CHART

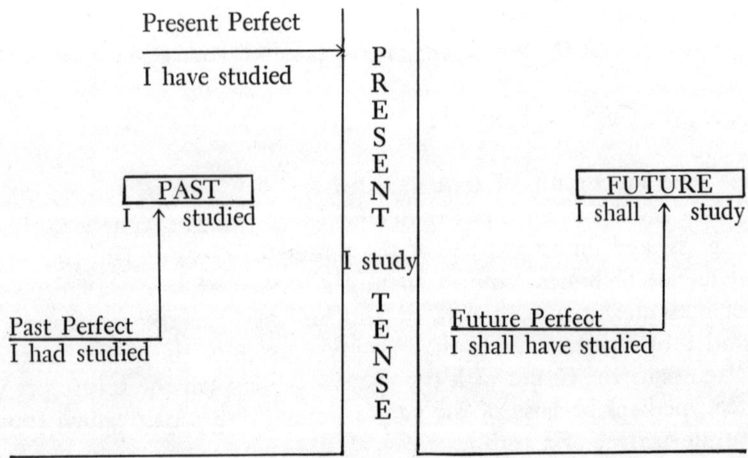

Examples:
> I had studied Social Science before I studied World Geography. (past perfect and past)
>
> I have studied International Law so I may take the Law exams. (present perfect and present)
>
> I shall have studied for twenty years when I shall receive my Ph.D. (future perfect and future)

AUXILIARY VERBS

To use tenses properly, the proper use of the auxiliary verbs, the helping verbs which indicate tense or time in English grammar, must be mastered. The auxiliary verbs—have, had, shall, will —which appear in the conjugations are not the only verbs which add to the verb meaning, so we _should_ examine other auxiliaries. We _shall_ begin with the derivation of "auxiliary." (Note the underlined words. WHY?) Auxiliary is derived from the Latin _auxilium_ (to aid, increase) + ary (suffix, relating to, connected with). This derivation explains the use of an auxiliary with the main verb of a sentence and indicates how it helps express the writer's thoughts and intentions more exactly.

The best procedure for studying auxiliaries is to record the dictionary definition beside each of the auxiliaries listed below and then provide a sentence containing a main verb of your choice and an appropriate auxiliary to increase the power of the verb:

can	could
may	might
should	must
would	ought

This discussion of auxiliaries requires reference to two other tenses of English verbs not usually included in a conjugation. These are the _progressive_ and _emphatic_ tenses. The names imply the purpose of each, neither of which is often used in all tenses of the verb. A synopsis will illustrate. Infinitive: to write

Progressive   *Emphatic*

Present: I am writing   Present: I do write
Past: I was writing   Past: I did write
Future: I shall be writing
Present Perfect: I have been writing
Past Perfect: I had been writing
Future Perfect: I shall have been writing

The *progressive* tenses introduce the verb *to be* as an auxiliary, and this leads to the discussion of an important use of *to be*, namely a characteristic of verbs not even mentioned up to this point: the *voice* of verbs.

Voice—Active and Passive

The *voice* of a verb shows the connection between the subject of the sentence and the verb. So far as the subject of the sentence is concerned that "connection" or relation is one of being *active* or *passive*, hence, the name of each voice.

Up to this point all discussion and examples of verbs have been in the active voice where the subject of the sentence was doing the action implied by the verb. Let us first examine the relationship between the active and passive voice subjects, verbs, and objects and then develop a synopsis of a verb in the passive voice.

The idea of *action* is important, so it is obvious that a passive voice verb must be a verb of action, a *transitive* verb, and not an *intransitive* verb. Compare these sentences and diagrams:

Sentence	*Diagram*			*Voice*
Lightning struck the tree.	Lightning (doer)	struck (action)	tree (receiver)	active
The tree was struck by lightning.	tree (receiver)	was struck (action)	by lightning (doer)	passive

Examine these sentences and note that:

1. In the *active voice* sentence the lightning (subject or *doer*) acts upon the tree (receiver).

2. In the *passive voice* sentence tree (subject or receiver) is acted upon by the lightning (doer).
3. A form of the verb *to be* has become the *auxiliary* of the passive voice.

A SYNOPSIS OF *to strike* IN THE PASSIVE VOICES

Principal parts: strike   struck   struck (3rd person singular)

Active voice	*Passive voice*
Present: It strikes	Present: It is struck
Past: It struck	Past: It was struck
Future: It will strike	Future: It will be struck
Present Perfect: It has struck	Present Perfect: It has been struck
Past Perfect: It had struck	Past Perfect: It had been struck
Future Perfect: It will have struck	Future Perfect: It will have been struck

Parallel Construction

Parallel construction is one of many ways to bring organization to your compositions, speeches, general communications. Parallel construction of verbs adds clarity and conciseness to directions and to organized writing. Here is an example of verbs in parallel construction to serve as a review of your study of this text. By this time you have:

Read the text thoughtfully.
Compared information on grammar with your knowledge and needs.
Corrected errors in your speech and writing.
Added to your understanding of words and your vocabulary.
Related ideas to develop your thinking.
Examined quotations for thought value and sentence structure.
Recognized grammatical constructions not otherwise pointed out.
Found grammar principles and style to study in depth in a handbook.
Considered ideas for writing of paragraphs, compositions, and research-length essays.

Checked off your use of various paragraph patterns.

Discovered that the dictionary is a valuable tool to be used constantly.

For further study of parallel construction turn to pages 184 to 188. A glance at the basic diagram of the poem "If (For Seniors)" will show that the poem is based on parallel construction, which gives not only organization, but also conciseness to the poem. Either now or later, when you are ready for the Final Review, study the grammatical forms which are used in parallel in the poem and which the review requires you to analyze.

Begin to use this form of communication of ideas in your thinking as well as your writing.

Note also in the excerpt on page 217 the way in which four infinitives summarize the agreed procedure of the Hazen Foundation Conference report of Colloquium III. (*Colloquium* is the Latin word for conversation.) The report says they agreed _to share_, _to continue_, and _to endeavor to create_. You recognize that all underlined words are infinitives. Further study of this sentence, which follows, will illustrate the power and value of using *verbals* and *verbal phrases* in your writing.

> At the conclusion of our deliberations we have agreed to share our thoughts and convictions through a series of publications, to continue our inquiries in various specific ways through the Study Groups and in new regional intergroup programs and to endeavor to create channels of communication with other concerned individuals and groups.

Verbals

In addition to acting like and looking like a verb, verbals act like other parts of speech. For instance, the *participle* is a verbal-adjective, the *gerund* is a verbal-noun, and the *infinitive* may be a verbal-adjective, -noun, or -adverb. The use in the sentence, of course, determines the part of speech. A verbal looking-like one part of speech and acting-like another reminds one of a "Genealogy Chart." How much can you learn about verbals from the following?

GENEALOGY CHART OF VERBALS

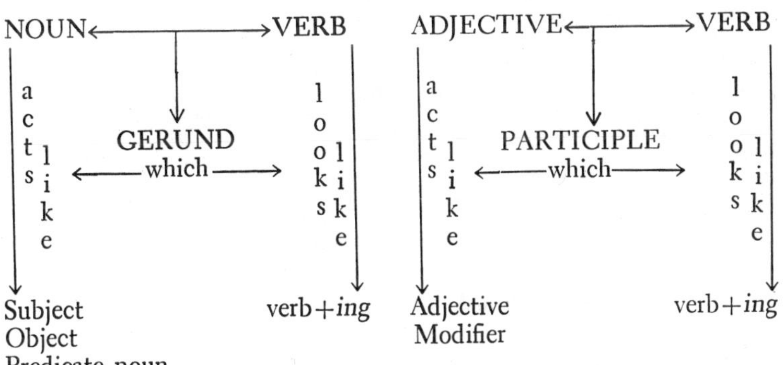

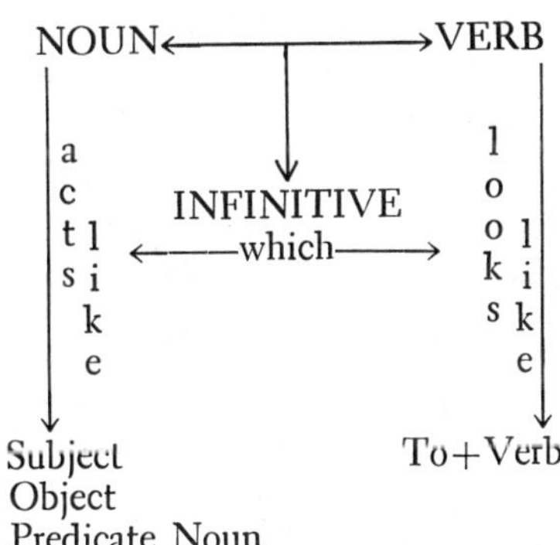

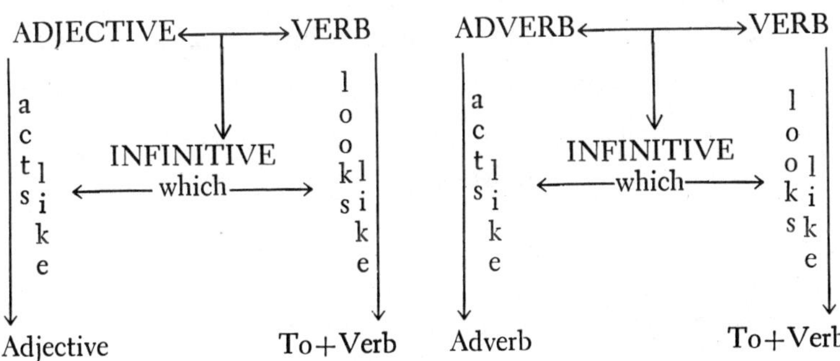

Verbals are often verbal *phrases* and, therefore, show characteristics of both "ancestors."

A study of the sentence from Colloquium III used in the preceding section of parallel construction will be helpful. The main part of the sentence is:

<pre>
                                    to share
                                    to continue
                                    to endeavor
          We   have agreed   to create
</pre>
(All infinitives are nouns used as direct objects)

In this sentence each infinitive is also part of a phrase and so the the infinitive shows verb as well as the noun characteristics of being the DO of the main verb in the sentence. Study the verbal qualities of each of the infinitives which are used as nouns and DO in the sentence:

<pre>
                       DO
      to share   our thoughts and convictions (HOW?) "through a
</pre>
series of publications" (adverb phrase)

<pre>
                       DO
      to continue   our inquiries (HOW?) "in various specific ways"
</pre>
"through the study Groups" and "in new regional inter-group programs" (adverb phrases)

<pre>
                       DO
      to endeavor   to create (another infinitive: How is this used?)
</pre>

<pre>
                       DO
      to create   channels (WHAT?) "of communication" "with
</pre>
other concerned individuals and groups" (adjective phrases)

Examples of Verbals

1. *Seeing is believing.*   (gerund as subject and predicate noun)

2. His *disobeying* the rules cannot be ignored.*   (gerund as subject)
3. The man *counting* the money is the treasurer.   (participle as adjective)
4. The pilot, *flying* into the airport in a rainstorm, said the landing would be routine.   (participle phrase as adjective)
5. She seems *to be intelligent*.   (infinitive phrase as predicate adjective)
6. *To think* is *to respect* yourself.   (infinitive as subject and predicate nominative)
7. He was given five books *to read*.   (Infinitive as adverb)

Now turn to the THOUGHT PROVOKER pages listed and determine how each verbal is used.

1. The great end of education is *to discipline* rather than *to furnish* . . .   (page 11)
2. *To listen* well is as powerful . . .   (page 53)
3. . . . the greatest art in life is *to have* as many pleasant thoughts as possible . . .   (page 73)
4. *To join thinking* with *reading* is . . .   (page 73)
5. . . . . efficient instrument in *thinking*   (page 31)
6. *Thinking*, not growth, makes manhood.   (page 73)

PREPOSITIONS
Latin prae (before) + ponere (to place)

In the section "A Conversation About Language" the point was made that homo sapiens had demonstrated intelligence when he had NEED of a prepositional word to relate one idea, or subject, with another. The "relationship" word is the preposition because it is pre-positioned (placed in front of) the idea or object which is related in some specific manner to another word in the sentence.

---

*Note: the possessive case of the pronoun is correct as the subject of the gerund; "rules" is the object of the gerund.

The preposition plus the noun or pronoun which follows, called the object of the preposition, is known as a prepositional phrase and is used as either an adjective or adverb in the sentence. In other words, the prepositional phrase answers one of the questions familiar to journalists:

Who? What? When? Where? Why? How?

There are two ways to determine whether the phrase is adverbial or adjectival—both are related. One is to determine which of the journalists' questions the phrase answers with regard to the word in the sentence to which the phrase is related. The other is to determine the part of speech of the word so modified.

Who? or What? are the questions answered by the adjective phrase, and the word modified would be a noun or pronoun.

The other questions are adverbial, and the word modified would be verbs, adjectives, or other adverbs.

There are more prepositions in English than in most of the parent languages. One reason is that the extra cases found in the parent languages were expressed by prepositional phrases when they came into the English language. Perhaps another reason is that, borrowing from so many languages, English could take on the "relating" qualities of them all. In many of the parent languages one preposition became translated into several more specific words in English. For instance, Latin has the preposition *ab*, which means *from*, *with*, or *by*, and *ad* which is translated *to* or *for*. An abundance of prepositions to select from allows English to express exact relationships.

What are some of these prepositions? Students taught me an interesting method of determining prepositions. "A preposition," they said, "is anything that an airplane can do to a cloud." Looking out a Florida classroom window, it was usually possible to *see a preposition* as an airplane would go

into	between
around	out of
above	toward
through	beside
under	away from

the clouds. The relationship of cloud and airplane was immediately understood, and it made prepositions seem to speak to them from the written page.

Let them speak to you! Turn to page 31 to the Thought Provokers on the subject of language. You will find an abundance of prepositional phrases, both adverbial and adjectival. Examples:

Phrase	Question Answered	Kind of Phrase
vehicle *of thought*	What?	Adjective
speech *in their dumbness*	What?	Adjective
grows *out of life*	Where? How?	Adverb
no tracing . . . *but by language*	How?	Adverb

Find other phrases on this page, but don't be fooled by the word "about" in the last comment on the page. Use your dictionary to determine how it is used in this sentence.

Now read over other Thought Provokers for phrases to analyze.

MODIFIERS
Latin modus (measure) + facere (to make)

The order in which the English parts of speech have been discussed in this book is purposeful. Sections on nouns, pronouns, verbs, and then prepositions have provided the "word tools" for thinking. Now we are ready to study modifiers and how the tools are used in sentences to communicate our thoughts—and communicate them accurately. This is the crux of the language problem, and studying modifiers will help us analyze the elements of the problem.

Let us begin, as in other discussions, with both derivations and definitions of the modifiers which include *adjectives, adverbs,* and *conjunctions,* to which words like clause, phrase, subordinate, coordinate, correlative, predicate, and subject must be added. These words must be defined and understood, for they are the vocabulary of man *thinking.*

A good exercise will now be for you to find the derivation of each of the words for yourself by selecting from the appropriate Latin parts, which are listed alphabetically below, and so create your own definitions. Turn to your dictionaries to check results only after you have seen what you can do to judge the derivations for yourself.

Use these derivations to define the vocabulary words. Note that there are more derivations than vocabulary words.

Example: predicate = *prae* (before) + *dicare* (to say).

Derivations in Latin	Vocabulary Words
	adjective
ad (to)	adverb
clausus, past participle of *claudere* (to close)	clause
com, also *co, con, cor* (with)	conjunction
dicare, akin to *dicere* (to say) (to proclaim)	coordinate
jacere (to throw)	correlative
jungare (to join)	
ordinare (to arrange) (to order)	phrase
phrasis (Greek *phrasis*<*phrazein*) (to speak)	predicate
prae (see preach) (before)	subject
relatus, past participle of *referre* (to bring back)	subordinate
sub (under)	word
verbum (word)	

For reference, you should have at hand the *definitions* of three new grammar terms:

PHRASE: in grammar, a sequence of a few words conveying a single thought or forming a separate part of a sentence but not containing a separate predicate.

CLAUSE: a group of words containing a subject and verb; part of a compound or complex sentence; when it is a dependent clause, it functions as a noun, adjective, or adverb. An independent clause is the main statement of the sentence.

PREDICATE: the word or words that make a statement about the subject of a clause or sentence; a predicate may be a verb and adverb, a transitive verb and object, a linking verb and complement.

Words, Including Verbals, As Adjectives and Adverbs

Review the jingle definition of adjectives and adverbs and apply the definitions to single words as examples. *Add the facts:*

1. Adjectives modify nouns and pronouns; this includes the gerund.
2. Adverbs modify verbs, adjectives and other adverbs, including participles and infinitives.
3. Adverbs often end in *ly*.
4. Both adjectives and adverbs have a comparative and superlative form.
5. The comparative adjective usually ends in *er* and the superlative in *est*.
6. The adverbs use *more* and *most* in the comparative and superlative.
7. Some adjectives are irregular in form. Check the dictionary if needed.
8. Don't be careless and use an adjective instead of an adverb.
9. Do check to see what kind of word the modifier belongs with and choose your word accordingly.
10. Review A Conversation About Language, page 35.

Examples:

		Comparative	Superlative
Adjectives:	good	better	best
	slow	slower	slowest
	sincere	sincerer	sincerest
	(or)	more sincere	most sincere
	pretty	prettier	prettiest
	far	farther	farthest
	far	further	furthest
Adverbs:	slowly	more slowly	most slowly
	sincerely	more sincerely	most sincerely
	carefully	more carefully	most carefully

Adjective and Adverb Phrases Examined

Page 146 in the section on verbs shows the line diagram for a *simple sentence*:

- - - - - _______

Now we must examine compound and complex sentences both by diagram and by word construction. A *compound sentence* would be diagramed:

- - - - - - ___________ and - - - - - - ___________

Indirect objects, IO, direct objects, DO, predicate nouns (or nominatives), PN, and predicate adjectives, PA, would do nothing to change these simple sentences joined by a conjunction. Even if phrases ( )were in the sentences they would still be simple sentences joined by a conjunction to form a compound sentence:

( )
- - - - - - ___________( ) and - - - - - -( )- ___________

Review the definition of *phrase* and note that there is no predicate in a phrase. The phrases indicated in the diagram above could be *adjective* or *adverb* phrases according to whether each modifies a noun or pronoun (adjectival); or modifies a verb, adverb, or adjective (adverbial).

Examine the list of prepositions and the example of prepositional phrases on page 163 then turn to the Thought Provokers on page 99. Note the quotation by Dr. Donald Andrews. The main part of this sentence, the independent clause, is:

Our knowledge of the atom brings us new hope.

(_______)   IO   DO
- - - - - - - - - - - - - - - - - - ___________

The prepositional phrases, in the complete sentence, the word modified, and the kind of phrases are:

1. (of the atom) describes *knowledge* so it is an adjective phrase.
2. (for a deeper understanding) modifies *hope*, DO, and is adjectival.
3. (of ourselves) and (of our world problems) both modify *understanding* and are adjectival.

In the remainder of the quotation find the following phrases and check what each modifies, the kind of phrase, and the question answered:

1. (inside the atom) modifies *can look* (adverbial, answers *where?*)
2. (beyond the material) modifies *something* (adjectival, answers *what?*)
   NOTE: does this last phrase describe *something* or tell *where?*
3. (through to a new horizon) modifies *see* (adverbial, answers question *where?*)
4. (of the spirit) modifies *horizon* (adjectival, answers question *what?*)

Adjective, Adverb, and Noun Clauses Examined

When a dependent clause is added to a sentence, there is a change in the sentence form from simple to complex. Review the definition of *clause* to familiarize yourself with the difference between an independent and a dependent clause. You will see that the *independent clause* is the same as a simple sentence and that the dependent clause, of whatever kind, produces a complex sentence by adding another subject and predicate to the main thought. A complex sentence diagram would be:

A. ______________________________________ adjective clause

B. (- - - —————) - - - ———————————— adverb clause

C. - - - - - ———————————— (- - —————) noun clause
                                               DO

The sentences for each of the above diagrams are:

A. The same experiments (which are giving us atomic power)
    -
    are also giving us atomic vision. Clause modifies ex-
    ————————————————————
                        IO   DO
    periments.

B. (As we develop our mental processes), we may become
    -
    more mature.
    ————————————
         PA

    Note the comma. This clause modifies the main verb.

C. All the evidence shows (that he was the guilty one).
    - - - - - - - - -   ————————————————————
                                      DO

    The clause is used as a noun, object of *shows.*

Punctuation is important with adverbs whether they are words, phrases, or clauses. Watch for the explanation of the comma in sentence B' in the review of punctuation. There will be more discussion about the punctuation of clauses under Punctuation.

Subordinate Conjunctions

Subordinate conjunctions introduce adverbial clauses:

because	as long as
since	though

<table>
<tr><td>although</td><td>before</td></tr>
<tr><td>as soon as</td><td>after</td></tr>
<tr><td>if</td><td>in order</td></tr>
<tr><td>so that</td><td>as</td></tr>
<tr><td>whereas</td><td>as if</td></tr>
<tr><td>when</td><td>that</td></tr>
<tr><td>while</td><td>until</td></tr>
<tr><td>where</td><td>unless</td></tr>
</table>

Relative Pronouns

Relative pronouns do just what the name implies—they relate to a specific noun in the sentence at the same time that they introduce the dependent clause used as an adjective clause.

Who, whose, whom relate to people, and, as you may have guessed, are the nominative, possessive, and objective forms as given. Thus it is important to know how the relative pronoun is *used in the clause* in order to select the proper case form.

Which, what, that are relative pronouns that usually refer to things rather than people.

PUNCTUATION

READING maketh a full man; conference a ready man; and writing an exact man; and, therefore, if a man write little, he had need have a great memory; if he confer little, he had need have a present wit; and if he read little, he had need have much cunning, to seem to know that he doth not.

Bacon

Think as well as READ, and when you read, yield not your minds to the passive impressions which others may make upon them. Hear what they have to say; but examine it, weigh it, and judge for yourselves. This will enable you to make a right use of books—to use them as helpers, not as guides to your understanding; as counsellors, not as dictators of what you are to think and believe.

Tryon Edwards

> *By READING, we enjoy the dead; by conversation, the living; and by contemplation, ourselves. Reading enriches the memory; conversation polishes the wit; and contemplation improves the judgment. Of these, reading is the most important, as it furnishes both the others.*
>
> COLTON

> *The WRITER does the most who gives his reader the most knowledge, and takes from him the least time.*
>
> SYDNEY

> *It has taken me years of struggle, hard work and research to learn to make one simple gesture, and I know enough about the art of WRITING to realize that it would take as many years of concentrated effort to write one simple, beautiful sentence.*
>
> ISADORA DUNCAN

> *Everything which I have created as a poet has had its origin in a frame of mind and a situation in life; I never WROTE because I had, as they say, found a good subject.*
>
> HENRIK IBSEN

Perhaps it seems strange to preface a review of punctuation by comments on reading and writing. However, when you consider that the inflection of the voice "punctuates" thoughts, and that thoughts are often written and rewritten in order to gain accuracy and precision, then the black marks one uses take on important and unique value.

You must conclude, therefore, that it is the WRITER'S OBLIGATION to use punctuation carefully and meaningfully. Up to now, you have read the quotations as Thought Provokers for ideas or sentence structure. Now, as you reread for punctuation, you will gain more insight into the quotation and will understand how grammatical construction and punctuation work together to help the author express his thoughts accurately.

Reviewing the marks of punctuation, we can take care of the period, question mark and exclamation point by saying that the basic statement—the subject, verb and complement—in the sentence either states a fact which requires a period (.), asks a question which requires a question mark (?), or exclaims something which requires an exclamation point (!). Other uses of the period can be found in your dictionary or your English handbook.

Commas

Before you review the quotations for careful comma punctuation analysis, we will review, as briefly as possible, the uses for the comma. We shall begin by simplifying the rules of punctuation and by studying the relationship between the basic statement of the sentence and the modifying (adjective or adverb) words, phrases, or clauses in the sentence.

First find the basic thought of the sentence by marking the subject, verb, and complement in some manner, or by noting them mentally. Next determine what the other elements in the sentence are and how each is used. Remember that the characteristic word order of English grammar is subject, verb, complement and that the complement may be the direct object (DO), the predicate noun (PN), or the predicate adjective (PA). Adjectives as words, phrases, or clauses may be found in either the subject or predicate of the sentence, and each will be modifying a noun or pronoun.

Adjectives used in a series to modify a noun will be punctuated as any series:

He was courageous, faithful, and candid.

Adjectives which are not restrictive are separated from the sentence by commas:

The winner, whoever he is, must collect the trophy immediately.

Most adjective clauses are restrictive and, therefore, are necessary, so no commas are needed:

Everything which I have created as a poet has had its origin in a frame of mind and a situation in life.

A comma may be used to indicate the omission of words in a sentence:

By reading, we enjoy the dead; by conversation, the living; and by contemplation, ourselves.

Now, having marked the subject, verb, and complement in the sentence with a pencil or mentally, and having noted all adjectival words, phrases, or clauses, you will note that whatever is left in the sentence is adverbial. Each remaining element tells How, When, Where, or Why about a verb, adjective, or adverb in the sentence. (Review the Parts of Speech jingle at this point if you need to.) The adverbs remaining in the sentence may be words, phrases, or clauses and will often need punctuation.

Introductory adverbs usually are punctuated in the following manner:

Too often, we limit our own accomplishments.
From our own experiences, we can often form judgments.
When he makes the decision, you will be the first to be told.

Parenthetical adverbial words, phrases, or clauses require two commas to set the adverbial off from the rest of the sentence. Only one comma would be an error because it would separate the subject from the verb in the sentence. Two commas have the effect of separating the parenthetical words from the main sentence parts:

This outcome, it should be noted, was not the result of scientific experimentation.

A new transportation system, at wonderful savings in time and gasoline, has just been developed.

By changing the word order of the sentence above, no comma is necessary:

A new transportation system has been developed at a wonderful savings in time and gasoline.

One exception to the rule that adverbial ideas appearing at the end of a sentence do not require punctuation can be illustrated by reference to one of the quotations at the beginning of this section. When the words *since, as,* or *for* are used in the sense of because, a comma should precede the word. The final sentence in the Colton quotation reads:

Of these, reading is the most important, as it furnishes both the others.

Semicolon and Colon

The semicolon is a very useful mark of punctuation. Some writers consider it to be a formal mark of punctuation and prefer the use of the dash (—). But both the dash and semicolon can have similar uses, so we will consider the semicolon here.

The semicolon (;) can be defined as a punctuation mark which functions as a *strong comma* or a *weak period*. There are several semicolons in the quotations on the punctuation page. All of them would be considered *weak periods* in usage: In the first quotation, the word "maketh" has been omitted from the second and third groups of words. Read the sentence with this word added and you see that the entire quotation is a series of three simple sentences and then three complex sentences. The semicolon has been chosen to give unity, compactness, and strength to the quotation.

The semicolon as a *strong comma* can be seen ten times in the poem "If (For Seniors)" on page 184. There the semicolon is the only possible mark of punctuation to indicate the difference in the comma at the end of each *if* clause which already has several commas in the four-line verse which makes up the entire *if* clause.

The colon (:) is used to indicate that words, phrases, clauses, or sentences will follow.

USING SENTENCE STRUCTURE TOOLS
AND ADDING PUNCTUATION

Sentence Structure Tools

Subjects * Predicates * Phrases * Clauses * Direct Objects * Indirect Objects * Predicate Nouns * Predicate Adjectives (Simple, Compound, Complex, and Compound-Complex sentences)

Review the Thinking Chart on page 126 and the last page of the "Conversation About Language" realizing that you are now studying syntax—the orderly or systematic arrangement of words as elements in a sentence to show their relationship—sentence structure, th.

Punctuation also plays a part in designating thought values and the relationships of ideas from one part of the sentence to another. So you must first know the grammar of the sentence before you can punctuate it.

This time when you review a quotation for Sentence Structure Study, also note the punctuation of the sentences. Ask yourself if the punctuation helps you understand the grammatical construction. It should.

Review of Tools in Use

The following sentences, or parts of sentences, illustrate important grammatical constructions. The diagrams correspond to that part of the sentence given here. Check the source for the entire quotation to see what else you can observe. Sentences not given page numbers are from the Buckminster Fuller article, so you can locate them easily.

Sentence	Diagram	Page
That word was synergy.	- - - - - ___________ PN	Bucky
Bucky was undismayed by such failures.	- - - - - ___PA ( )___	Bucky
He kept planning his dirigible house.	- - - - - ___________ DO	Bucky
I'll see that Marshall Field and Company patents it in your name. (*Note:* the clause is a noun clause, DO of *see.*)	- - - - - ___[- - - ——DO( )]___	Bucky
The specialist took things apart but the architect put things together.	- - - - - ——————DO——————but ————DO———	Bucky
Bucky had a favorite way of describing the state	- - - - - ___DO ( )___	Bucky
I am sorry when any language is lost. (*Note:* the PA is modified by adverb clause.)	- - - - - ___PA(- - - - ——)___	31
*The family that does not take . . . at least one newspaper. . . . (*Note:* this portion of the sentence is the subject with an adjective clause modifying the noun.)	N (- - - - ___DO___)	87
. . . cosmos which we know scientifically to exist . . . (*Note:* this portion of the sentence is a clause with an infinitive as the DO of the verb in the clause—the entire portion is part of the noun clause object of *find* in the sentence.)	___DO Inf.___ (- - - ——————)	99
. . . give an account of itself at your breakfast table. (*Note:* this portion of the predicate has two phrases—one modifies the DO so is adjectival, the other is adverbial modifying *give* and telling *where.*)	___DO ( ) ( )___	87

---

*When a portion of a sentence is omitted use three dots (. . .) to indicate omission. If the omission comes at the end of the sentence, add a fourth dot (. . . .) as the period in the sentence.

When you turned to the quotations from which these sentences were taken, I hope you found many other interesting grammar illustrations to study. This should give you an idea of how well the language tools work together to communicate thoughts precisely.

NOW, take the General Sentence Structure Review Test which follows by matching the sentences, numbered 1 to 22, with the diagrams, lettered A to V. An answer chart is on page 184. Be prepared to review back pages whenever necessary, but do not turn to the answers until you have conquered all.

GENERAL SENTENCE STRUCTURE REVIEW TEST

Match sentences 1 to 22 with diagrams A to V. Answers are on page 184.

1. American history is very interesting.
2. They had become the idols of the general public.
3. No amount of reasoning alone will develop conversational ability.
4. He answered her cleverly with an original pun.
5. For many years the lighthouse has warned the ships at sea of countless perils of fog and storm.
6. People who ask personal questions are seldom welcome callers.
7. He wants to continue his schooling where he can specialize in music.
8. The current craze was philately or stamp collecting.
9. What annoyed him most were my sudden summer plans which did not include him.
10. He charged and I took off cross-country.
11. Above the table, battle flags were hung and a fireplace of carved marble was decorated.
12. Objectives of the organization were explained at the meeting and printed copies were distributed.
13. Our hearing which occurs with lightning speed is registered as soon as vibrations hit the eardrums.
14. The likelihood is that everybody has psi.

15. The speaker of the occasion who had known her all his life cited her as someone to be emulated.
16. His giving me an explanation of their plan was an unexpected move.
17. The plane landed and immediately the dignitaries descended.
18. He has never played a note since he lost his grandfather's treasured Stradivarius.
19. Those who enjoy great literary masterpieces can easily extend this pleasure.
20. The grammatical structure of the Spanish language resembles that of French and both are considered Romance languages.
21. At the general business meeting he read the names, and the candidates for each position were introduced.
22. The girl between those boys who are wearing varsity sweaters is my daughter whom you have met.

DIAGRAMS

(Match the letter to the number of the sentence)

Key: - - - - - - - -   Subject of Sentence
        _________   Predicate of Sentence
        (   )   Phrase
        (- - - ___)   Clause
            &   Conjunction/Compound Sentence

A.    ( )   ( )

B.    (- - - ___)   PN (- - - ___ DO)

C. 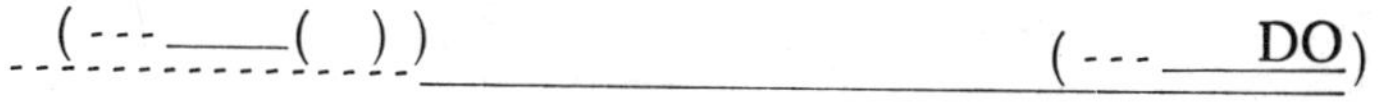   (- - - ___ ( ))   (- - - ___ DO)

D.

E.

F.

G.

H.

I.

J.

K.

L.

M.

N.

O.

P.

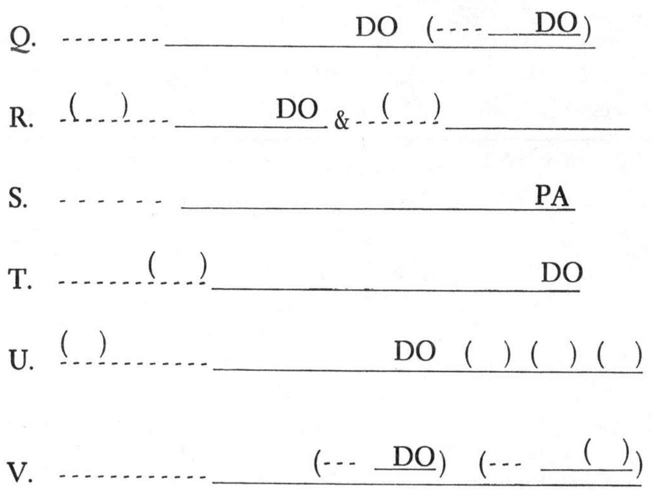

Q. -------- _______________ DO (---- ___DO___)

R. .(...)... _________ DO & .(...)._________

S. - - - - - - ___________________________ PA

T. ----------(...)_____________________ DO

U. (..)____________________ DO ( ) ( ) ( )

V. ------------_________ (--- ___DO___) (--- ____(..)____)

Note: In the diagrams above there are simple, compound, and complex sentences.

The sentences include:

Noun clauses (used as subject, predicate noun, object)
Adjective clauses
Adverbial clauses (answering the W's)
Prepositional phrases as adjectives or adverbs
Infinitive phrases
Participial phrases

COMPARISON OF SENTENCE STRUCTURES

Review the history of English, the borrowed language, page 128.

Recall references to Latin derivations for English words throughout the book.

Remind yourself of the order of an English sentence—subject, verb, complement and adverb.

Examine the English sentence which has been translated into several different languages. This study will indicate to you that every language has its own grammar and sentence structure.

An "educated guess" will give you a little idea of the variation of word order in the several languages.

This interesting study came to be through an unusual conversation I had with a traveling companion who had lived in several countries after leaving her homeland in Holland. She was interested in the comparative language study I proposed adding to *The Art of Communication: A Self-Help Course in Basics,* and generously supplied six different language translations.

We begin with the English sentence used in each translation and then the Latin teacher's translation.

ENGLISH:
The person who knows the grammar of his mother tongue can learn a foreign language easily.

LATIN:
Homo qui grammaticam sui patrii sermonis scit barbaram linguam discere facile potest.

DUTCH:
Hy die de spraakkunst van zyn landstaal kent leert gemakkelyk een vreemde taal.

GERMAN:
Der Mann der die Grammatik seiner Muttersprache kennt kann eine fremde Sprache leicht lernen.

CASTILIAN SPANISH:
Aquel que domina la gramatica de su lengua madre puede aprender cualquier otra idioma mas facilmente.

FRENCH:

Celui qui connâit bien la grammaire de sa langue natale apprend facilement une langue étrangère.

ITALIAN:

Una persona che sa la grammatica che ha imparato dallasua madre puo facilmente imparare qualsiasi lingua.

INDONESIAN:

Orang jang tahu ilmu nahu dan saraf bahasa ibu bisa beladjar dengan mudah bahasa asing.

The French teacher added the following comments:
In French, adjectives and adverbs often come *after* the noun.

Examples of differences in French and English grammar:

1. A friend of mine
   Un de mes amis
2. Whose bag is this?
   A qui est ce sac?
3. I gave them to him.
   Je les lui ai donné. (pronoun comes before the verb)
4. What do Americans do on the 30th of May?
   Que font les Americains le trente mai?
5. I cannot do it.
   Je ne peux pas le faire. (Half the negative comes before the
   verb and half after.)

A minister commented that in Greek the verb can be any-where in the sentence, while in ancient Hebrew the verb is the first word in the sentence. It is also interesting to note that ancient writings had no punctuation at all.

Answers for GENERAL SENTENCE STRUCTURE RE-
VIEW TEST
Pages 178-79.

1	S	12	N
2	I	13	C
3	T	14	O
4	J	15	D
5	U	16	P
6	K	17	E
7	V	18	Q
8	L	19	F
9	B	20	G
10	M	21	R
11	A	22	H

FINAL REVIEW

NOW combine all you have read and studied about parts of
speech, sentence structure, and punctuation.

USE this background to study the grammatical construction
of the poem "If (For Seniors)" which is patterned on the Kipling
poem. As in Kipling's poem, so in Helen Reed's, the last two
lines of the poem are the main clauses of the sentence. The
entire poem is one *compound-complex sentence.*

IF
(For Seniors)*

by Helen Reed

1. If you have learned mistakes are ways of learning
   That all will make, that teachers are your friends,

---

*Helen Reed, Librarian, Maimisburg, Ohio, from the *NEA Journal*,
March 1961. Used with permission. (This poem is valuable for sentence
and punctuation criticism and analysis.)

That they are best when they are most demanding,
And that your education never ends;

2. If you have learned that grades are rings on targets
Put there to help you really hit the mark,
And that if you're a cheater, you're the cheated
To turn from truth and light to choose the dark;

3. If you have learned that facts are tools of learning
To help you think, that judging is your aim
—To find the facts, then weigh in balanced measure
And count that good which has the better claim;

4. If you have learned that rules are made for reasons
The purpose being that they help us all,
And that the heart in youth will have its seasons
And like the tides of spring will rise and fall;

5. If you have learned to laugh, but not at others,
And to be clean in body, soul, and mind;
If you have learned that you best star in teamwork,
And most of all the gift of being kind;

6. If you have learned that you must serve to master
And having mastered, then you owe your best;
If you can smile when you have met disaster
And start to work again with greater zest;

7. If you have found all men are really brothers,
And that together we must rise or fall,
That he who does the most in helping others
Is at the last the greatest of us all;

8. If you regard your promise once it's given
As sacred as an altar's holy flame
And treasure most of all things under heaven
Your self-respect as well as your good name;

9. If you have learned that error's often lauded,
That truth is very difficult to find,
You will have earned that coveted diploma
And what is more, you'll have a well-trained mind.

The basic diagram of the SENTENCE would look like this:

          you   have learned
(If - - - - - - - ___________________________ . . .
                   . . . education never ends;)

          you   have learned
(If - - - - - - - ___________________________ . . .
                   . . . to choose the dark;)

          you   have learned
(If - - - - - - - ___________________________ . . .
                   . . . has the better claim;)
And so on for five more verses—THEN

          you   have learned
(If - - - - - - - - ___________________________ . . .
                   . . . difficult to find,)

     you   will have earned   diploma   (DO)
- - - - - - - - - - ____

     you   will have   mind   (DO)
- - - - - - - - - - ____ .

With this general pattern in mind, see how easily you can find the *clauses*, *phrases*, *verbals* listed below and tell yourself what kind each is and how each is used in the sentence. THEN go on to find many more constructions and give the reasons for each mark of punctuation.

(*Hint*: For the sake of rhythm, the word "that" is omitted from the first line and "mistakes" from the second. Add these words in the proper places and you will understand the construction better.)

GOOD LUCK   GOOD FUN   GOOD THINKING
as you find:

NOUN CLAUSES:

There are 5 in stanza 1. How is each used?

ADJECTIVE CLAUSE:

Consider "which has the better claim" in stanza 3.

PREDICATE ADJECTIVE:

Prove that "that they help us all" stanza 4 is a predicate adjective.

ADVERB CLAUSES:

"If you can smile when you have met disaster" in stanza 6 has two clauses. How is each used? What question does each answer.

How many *if* clauses are there all together?

Tell all you can about "As sacred as an altar's holy flame" in stanza 8.

PHRASES:

In stanza 2 find "on target," tell what kind of phrase it is, and what it modifies.

Also in stanza 2, "from truth" is used in what way? and what is "to turn?"

In stanza 4 tell all you know about "in youth."

Do the same for "in helping others" in stanza 7.

VERBALS:

Remember, infinitives are used as nouns, adverbs, adjectives; gerunds are nouns, and participles are adjectives.

In stanza 5, study "to laugh" for how it is used. In the same stanza study "to be."

"Of learning" is a gerund in stanza 3; "in helping" is a gerund in stanza 7.

"You" is understood as the pronoun that the participle "having mastered" modifies, in stanza 6.

The past participle in stanza 2 modifies "one," which is understood; "the cheated" is the participle.

PARAGRAPH WRITING

According to the Thinking Chart which introduces this section, we are now ready to consider the "size" thought represented by TH. A TH thought relates sentences with one idea to form a thought unit called a paragraph. Your dictionary indicates that the word *paragraph* comes from Greek, *para* (before or beside) and *graphein* (to write) and refers to either the mark which, when placed beside a sentence, indicates where a paragraph is to begin, or refers to the unit of thought which is separated by indenting the first line, or by omitting a line between the units of thought. Thus, TH represents a larger thought unit than any studied up to this point in the text.

You will now want to refer to the original paragraphs you have in your file folder. This time you will consider the interrelationship of sentences in each paragraph, and you will learn how to use the Paragraph Patterns in this section. At the end of this section, examples of paragraph models are indicated by essay and paragraph number. They are to be used for study just as the quotations on the division pages have been used for models to analyze sentence structure of your own sentences.

Be warned, however, that in the daily, practical writing you do, the paragraph-unit-idea must always be present to prove that you have organized your thinking. In a short business letter, the Who, What, When, Where, Why (the W's which also apply to newspaper writing) may be so "stretched out" for the businessman's ease and speed of reading that the separate would-be paragraphs are really the topic sentence, development, and conclusion of a single paragraph unit. Newspaper copy is another example of a "stretched-out" paragraph made up of headline, lead-in, body, and conclusion.

A good way to introduce paragraphs for study is by considering William Butler Yeats's "The Balloon of the Mind," which suggests that we bring the "balloon of the mind" into its "narrow shed," as a definition of a paragraph.

A freshman student developed his commentary on his English course in a paragraph, as follows:

We are being taught to use our own balloon; the one each of us was issued on our birthday. You want us each to appreciate our own balloon and learn to tie it with others so that the rig as a whole can lift more weight. Breezes carry the rig; just as opinion, criticism, moods, and interests carry our thoughts. Many relationships between the balloon and the mind have appeared to me. While discussing authors, scientists, and other famous people, I wonder if they and I use the same air in each of our balloons and how much my ten-cent carnival balloon could help somebody else's dirigible. Perhaps that little extra lift that my balloon has would be all it takes to get another's ship off the ground.

A Student

PARAGRAPH PATTERNS

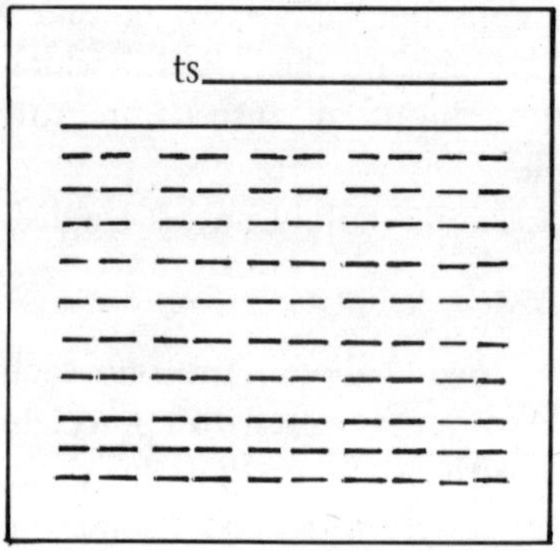

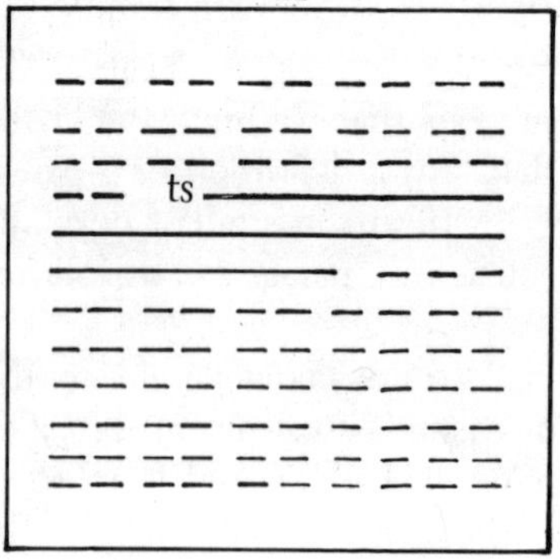

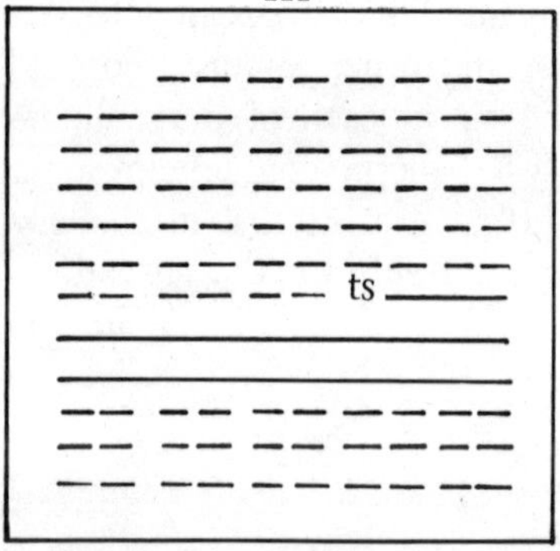

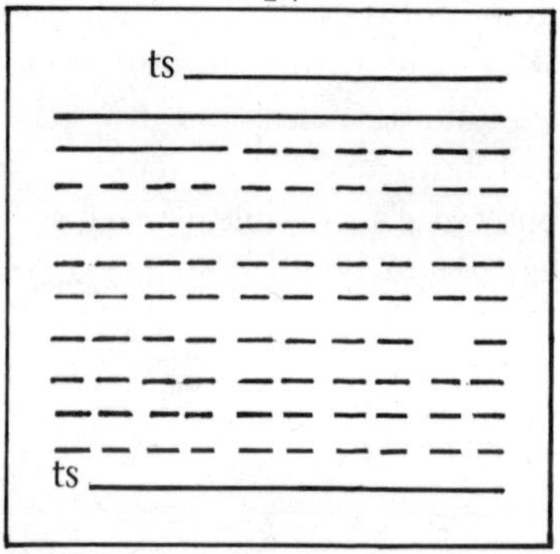

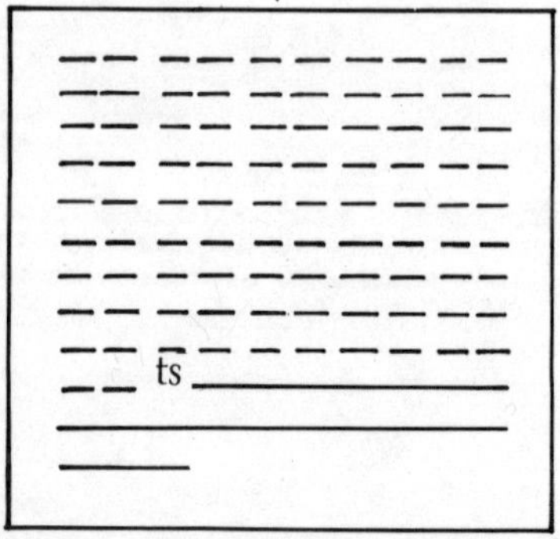

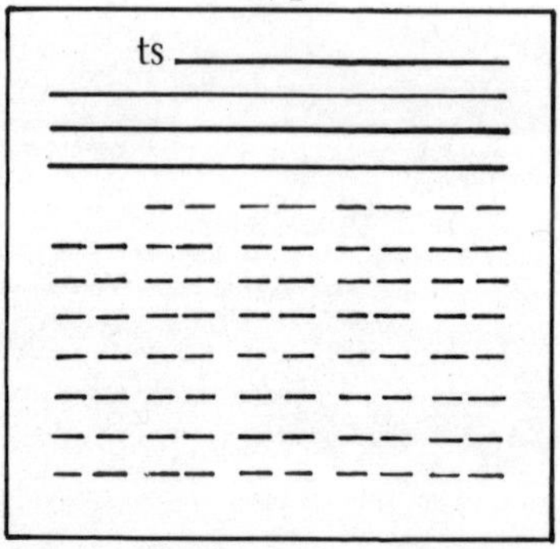

PARAGRAPHS IN A COM-POSITION:

ts ________ : topic sentence
- - - - - - - - - : development
x x x x x x x x: transitional ideas

Studying Paragraph Patterns

As noted on the Paragraph Patterns page, in each diagram
(*ts* _______) indicates the topic sentence, (- - - - - -), the development of the topic sentence, and (x x x x), the transitional
ideas. Before studying the diagrams carefully, it might be interesting and helpful to review the dictionary definition of inductive
and deductive reasoning, noting that the prefix *in* means from, and
de down. Some students may also want to review the section of a
logic text on inductive and deductive reasoning.

Examine the Paragraph Patterns on the preceding page, ask
yourself the following questions, and relate them and your answers
to individual patterns:

1. Does a number designation appearing in a *ts* which is first
   in a paragraph suggest what may be the purpose of the following sentences in the paragraph?
2. When the *ts* is second, what may be the purpose of the first
   sentence?
3. When the *ts* is in the middle of the paragraph, what may be
   the purpose of the first and last parts of the paragraph?
4. If a *ts* is outside a paragraph, may there be still other paragraphs relating to the same *ts*?
5. Why is it possible to have a paragraph without a *ts* specifically stated?

Now, get out your file folder with your accumulated paragraphs. If you have not already done so, find the topic sentence
in each of your paragraphs. Criticize your own writings in the
light of these paragraph patterns and determine to have better
organization, such as these patterns suggest, in all your future
writings.

Finally study the following paragraphs which, unless otherwise designated, have been taken with permission from "A War
on Fuzziness" by William Safire in the November-December,
1976 issue of *Todays Education*. Safire is a *New York Times*
columnist.

PATTERN I:

I suggest that this fuzziness is interrelated and is spreading. I want to show how it exists in my field, the world of words; how it has insidiously worked its way into the schools; and how it is now billowing out across the landscape of political ideas. Then, because I believe in precision, I will suggest how, together, we can launch a counterattack.

PATTERN IV:

Our vogue words are vague words. We are afflicted with the response of feeling rather than the response of understanding. Let me illustrate: About ten years ago, the standard response to everything was "Fantastic." As that murmured answer became popular, it was replaced by "Beautiful." Today, the standard response is "Terrific." The word is not a word; it is an approved sound to express not a thought but one's presence in the room. *A simple grunt would be a better use of language.*

PATTERN V:

The slang term *funky* had its origin in jazz lingo some forty years ago, when funky was said to be the odor of a stale cigar. Louis Armstrong used to play in a place called "Funky Butt Hall." Later, that adjective for the smell of cigars in jazz dives came to mean jazzy, and then avant garde, and now, modish, as applied to dress. *Students should know what the slang they use means and whence it is derived—this wakes up their curiosity about words.*

PATTERN III:

I know some educators insist that career education is a terrible trend toward vocational training at an early age and say that we must let our children be children. The answer to that is to let our children be people. Economics is a fact of real life,

and young people do well to learn fairly early about the dignity
of work and the discipline that careers demand. _We should not
be so embarrassed about stressing the value of getting ahead in
life by combining talent, training, and hard work._ Twenty-one is
certainly not the age for retirement.

PATTERN II:
(From _Wizard of the Dome_ by Sidney Rosen, page 45)

By 1959, more than a hundred companies had been licensed to
manufacture geodesic domes. Some of these were "plydomes,"
made of bent pieces of plywood and used as playhouses in parks
and playgrounds. _Others were huge affairs, costing as much as
two hundred thousand dollars each._ The Union Tank Car Company built and installed such a dome, three hundred and eighty-
four feet across, at Baton Rouge, Louisiana. This dome, which
could accommodate an entire football field and stadium, was
large enough for whole trainlengths of railroad cars that needed
rebuilding. A similar dome was built at Woods River, Illinois.
There was a geodesic dome over the Anheuser-Busch Park aviary
in Tampa, Florida, and another over that dolphin playground,
the Seaquarium, at Miami. . . . In addition to designing and
consulting fees, Bucky's corporations reecived five percent of the
sales price of every dome made by a licensed manufacturer.

PATTERN VI:
(From "New Bust in the Hall of Fame" by Wade Van Dore
page 111. Here the ts is outside the main paragraph.)

_However this may be, some of the new readers of Walden
and "Civil Disobedience" are going to have a hard time reconciling this man's so pointed life and words with prevalent lax
practices._
If Thoreau were here now, he would challenge our "economy
of abundance treadmill," as someone has called it, with his dear
creed of scarcity. He would repeat what he said a hundred years

ago that "things are in the saddle and ride mankind," and passionately urge us to "simplify, simply, simplify." He would remind us that "a man is rich in proportion to the number of things he can do without"; that the faculty of thought, or the ability to contemplate one's self and the grandeur of the universe, gives us deeper satisfaction and pleasure than material wealth.

Studying Paragraph Development

A topic sentence may be developed, or classified, by several different means. A brief list of the methods which may be used will here suffice. Reference to a dictionary for definitions of terms not familiar to you will be helpful.

The methods for developing topic sentences into paragraphs include:

1. Reasoning inductively or deductively
2. Comparing or contrasting ideas
3. Using an analogy
4. Using examples
5. Using quotations
6. Using repetition
7. Using details to support a statement

A combination of methods is also possible.

DIRECTIONS FOR STUDYING SPECIFIC PARAGRAPHS:

In addition to recognizing how paragraphs referred to below have been developed, underline the sentence you consider to be the topic sentence *and* indicate the pattern.

Think of each paragraph as a mini-composition: mini (small) com (with) posi (placed) tion (a suffix forming a noun).

Remember, it is more difficult to write a short, concise paragraph than a rambling, many-paragraphed composition. "I'm sorry this is so long; I did not have time to condense it," is sometimes a valid, and honest, excuse.

Unless otherwise noted, the following numbered references for examples of paragraph development are in "The Cultural Search for Meaning: Man, Youth and Values," beginning on page 217 of this text.

Study the punctuation as you read each paragraph:

1. Inductive: Paragraph A
2. Deductive: Paragraph B
3. Contrasting/comparing: Paragraph M
4. Analogy (see "The Language and Message of Walden," pages 114-15): Paragraph 4
5. Example: Paragraph C
6. Quotation: Paragraph H, J
7. Repetition: Paragraph C
8. Details: Paragraph L

For continuity between paragraphs (represented by x's in Paragraph Patterns), see paragraphs C, D, E, F, L, M, N for the following transitional ideas that connect the paragraphs:

"Still another. . . ."
"Another aspect. . . . We will become aware . . . of urgency . . . ways . . . and rebirth. . . ."
"These considerations. . . ."
"Finally, . . ."
"The problem is. . . ."
"What then is the problem. . . ."
"What is needed therefore. . . ."

ON THE ELASTIC MIND

THOUGHT PROVOKERS
AND
SENTENCE STRUCTURE STUDY

There is nothing so elastic as the human mind. Like imprisoned steam the more it is pressed the more it rises to resist the pressure. The more we are obliged to do, the more we are able to accomplish.

TRYON EDWARDS

A great thought is a great boon, for which God is to be first thanked, then he who is the first to utter it, and then, in a lesser but still in a considerable degree, the man who is first to quote it to us.

CHRISTIAN NESTELL BOVEE

The progress of democracy seems irresistible, because it is the most uniform, and the most ancient, and the most permanent tendency which is to be found in history.

DE TOCQUEVILLE

A KEY TO LIBRARY RESEARCHING*

Now, then, American Scholar, do you have the Key to your successful library researching?

Do you feel *confident, comfortable,* and *courageous* when you enter your college library or your community library? Do you know and respect the tools you will use to acquire the knowledge you seek?

Or does the silence of the library awe you and the sight of other students successfully using resource material they have found for themselves make you envious? Does the procedure for following their example confuse you?

If so, then you need some hints on appearing sophisticated while you learn the key to library usage and begin sharing its tools with others.

As soon as possible, spend two or three hours in your library by yourself following these hints.

1. Before entering the library, prepare small note cards as follows: On one write only the name of an *author;* on another the *title* of a book; on a third a *subject* on which you would like book references; on a fourth *another subject* which you know has been discussed in magazines.

2. Approach the card catalogue in your library with confidence. Select the proper alphabetical drawer for the first letter of the person's last name which your author card indicates. Find a card for this author and enter on your blank author card the title of a book written by him, the subject of the book, and the library call number which you will find in the upper left-hand corner. Follow this same procedure for the cards you have prepared for the title of a book and the subject on which you believe you will find books written. For the subject card, list several titles and call numbers for books on your subject that appeal to you.

3. Go to the book stacks and locate by call number the books you have identified by the above process. For this first get-acquainted library visit it is not necessary to do more than locate your books on the shelves.

---

*Dorothy Myers Peed, *America Is People and Ideas: Library Researching for the Space Age* (New York: Exposition Press, Inc., 1966), pp. 26-28.

4. Find the tables in your library where the *Reader's Guide to Periodical Literature Indexes* are available. Select a volume by the date which would logically have references on your chosen subject. (References to the astronauts would not appear in volumes before the late 1950s or 1960s.) Confidently select magazine references, being sure to include on your card all necessary information to locate the magazine in the stacks. Find the magazines you have chosen. The stacks are usually near the *Reader's Guide* table. Watch your confidence and courage grow with each successful "find."

5. Follow this same procedure (in 4 above) using the *New York Times Index* if you find that your college has this library service.

6. Return to the card catalogue and look up the word "dictionary." Note your gain in confidence as you handle the cards this time. Count the number of cards under "dictionary." Note the names of several you would like to examine; indicate the title and call number for each. Follow this same procedure for the word "encyclopedia."

7. Locate the Great Books of the Western World. In volume I see the Preface for what these books are about.

8. Now tour the Reserve Books area, simply looking at the titles and varieties of references available. Locate the dictionaries and encyclopedias of special interest to you. Select one from the shelf and take it to a nearby table. Make yourself comfortable as you begin your quest for information on your chosen subject.

9. Before you leave the library this first time, glance in the periodicals room to learn where the daily newspapers are kept and the number of magazines available to you. Then note all special library displays and exhibits, promising yourself to return later on to study them in detail.

The key to library researching is now yours. It is up to you what you will do with it during your college years and on into adult life. Librarians are eager to assist you in your work, especially when they realize that you are bending every effort to master the use of the library on your own. Detailed guidebooks to the library are abundant and will be more understandable after this first exploratory visit. As you do the research required in various disciplines, you will possibly encounter frustrating experiences in your quest for information. But none will be devoid of some learning experience, and many may lead you into channels which you would never have considered exploring on your own. Says one young man about his first library study experience: "My researching took me to the library, which before this was simply a study hall in my freshman eyes: I chose several books and became so intrigued with my new knowledge that I almost forgot my purpose in reading. At last I found myself, began to organize my facts, and formulated my approach. When I completed my work, I was still a freshman; but in a new sense, for now I was a thinking, college student."

Education never ends. Here in the college library you are establishing habits of thought and study which you will carry into your adult community life. There in your local library, in addition to the books and reference material you have come to use with ease, you will probably find available to you lecture series, adult education class material, information to update your science knowledge, and, in literary books, generous reference to all phases of the humanities.

TOPICS FOR LIBRARY RESEARCHING*

The Scholar is that man who must take up unto himself all ability of the time, all the contributions of the past, all the hopes of the future. He must be a university of knowledge. If there be one lesson more than another which should pierce his ear, it is: The world is nothing, and you know not yet how a globule of sap ascends; in yourself slumbers the whole of Reason; it is for you to know all; it is for you to dare all . . . this confidence in the unsearched might of man belongs to all motives, by all prophecy, by all preparation, to the American Scholar.

RALPH WALDO EMERSON

The Maury-Draper family groups are used in this library-research study not only because they represent a vast and varied number of interests and accomplishments, but also because they are characteristic of their era, when rugged individualism was an accepted characteristic of American life. The automation and conformity of the twentieth century had not impressed on their generations the mold that, today, often prevents students from being curious about a multitude of subjects. They questioned, investigated, worked, and eventually demonstrated their findings in many fields. In doing so, they exemplified Emerson's belief that each man has it in him to contribute something to knowledge.

---

*Peed, *America Is People and Ideas*, pp. 169-173.

So varied is the even-incomplete list of the activities of several members of these families that students today can begin their search for a liberal education by investigating the subjects detailed in this section.

The topics are listed in subject groups that correspond with the work of members of the Maury and Draper families. In this way the student can keep before him the unity amid the diversity that these projects can have.

GENERAL SUBJECTS*

Astronomy

Astrophysics
Star Spectrum
Sun Spots
Doppler Principle
Draper Catalogue of Stars
Observatory, Hastings-on-Hudson
Daguerreotype of the Moon
Dr. Annie Cannon

Nebula of Orion
Planetarium
Telescopic Photography
Dr. Harlow Shapley
The Milky Way
Binary Stars
E. C. Pickering
William Bond
Copernicus and Galileo

Conservation and Ornithology

Soil Conservation
Water Conservation
Sequoias—Redwoods
President Theodore Roosevelt's Interest in Conservation
National Parks
American Eagle
John James Audubon Migrations

Water Birds to Everglades
Swallows to Capistrano
Monarch Butterflies to Pacific Grove, Calif.
Massachusetts Audubon Society
Local Audubon Tours
Key West Audubon Home
Winter Bird-Feeding

Oceanography

Matthew Fontaine Maury, Founder of Science of Oceanography
Scripps Institute of Oceanography
U.S. Oceanographic Fleet
Polaris Submarine and Oceanography
The Gulf Stream, a River of the Ocean
Plankton and Whales
Midshipman, Commodore, Professor, Matthew Fontaine Maury
Maury Holiday, Maury Lake, etc., in Virginia

---

*These subjects should suggest more recent ones to add to the list.

Photography

Louis Daguerre and the Daguerreotype
John William Draper Photographs the Moon
Celestial Photography
Satellite Photography

General Science

The Pickerings
    of Harvard Observatory—Astronomy
    of M.I.T.—Laboratory Sciences
Carlotta Maury, Paleontologist
Mytton Maury, Editor of *Geographic Magazine*
Antonia Maury, Astronomer
Albert Einstein (1879-1955)
    Autobiography
    Mathematics in Astronomy
    Theory of Relativity
John William Draper (1811-1882)
    Chemistry in Photography
    Chemistry in Medicine
    Radiant Energy
Henry Draper (1834-1882)
    Chemistry of Blood Cells
    Spectroscopy
International Geophysical Year (IGY), 1957-1958
    IGY Study of the Oceans
    IGY Study of the Earth
    IGY Study of the Sky
    IGY Study of the Weather
    IGY Study of the Sun and the Universe
International Years of the Quiet Sun (IGQSY)
    Studies made in 1964-1965
Modern Devices to Investigate and Measure Space
Moon Landing
Mars Landing

History

Vasco da Gama   Madison
Copernicus   Cyrus Field
Galileo   Maury Day in Virginia
Sir John Herschel   Draper Valley in Virginia
Samuel F. B. Morse   Space Flight and Astrophysics
Jefferson   Smithsonian Institution
Adams   Washington

*   *   *

As you begin the work which follows on researching, developing an idea, thinking, and writing, appreciate the fact that this is your right and privilege as a citizen of a democracy.

PREPARATION FOR YOUR RESEARCH EXPERIENCE

To be valuable and interesting for you, your researching must be creative. Study the following excerpts from a syllabus* of a successful Freshman English course, and wherever possible apply the ideas to your work and experiences.

OBJECTIVE OF THE COURSE

The objective of the 101-70's sections of the Communications Course at Palm Beach Junior College is to help students read and write with more accuracy, interest, effectiveness, and self-satisfaction. Though this course cannot be considered one in Creative Writing, it does purpose to help the student recognize his own individualized thoughts, realize that thoughts are expressed in single words or word groups, and determine the relationships of these thought groups, one to another; thus he more confidently expresses his ideas, however complicated, orally or in writing. The PROCEDURE is to have the student delineate a creative idea of his own which can be developed in some way through library reading and then communicated in acceptable written form as a research manuscript, knowing, all during the procedure, that he is establishing a study routine which will be duplicated many times and in many different courses during his college career.

OBJECTIVE, AS STATED BY OTHERS IN THE PAST AND THE PRESENT

By Ralph Waldo Emerson in his essays "The American Scholar" and "Intellect":

The Scholar is that man who must take up unto himself all the ability of the time, all the contributions of the past, all the hopes of the future. He must be a university of knowledge. . . .

---

*Dorothy Myers Peed, "English Syllabus for Freshman Communications," Palm Beach Junior College, Lake Worth, Florida, 1968. (The page numbers, unless otherwise indicated, have been altered to refer to pages in this text.)

All our progress is an unfolding like the vegetable bud. You have first an instinct, then an opinion, then a knowledge, as the plant has root, bud and fruit. Trust the instinct to the end, though you can render no reason. It is vain to hurry it. By trusting it to the end, it shall ripen into truth, and you shall know why you believe. Each mind has its own method. . . . In a moment and unannounced, the truth appears, and is the distinction, the principle we wanted. But the oracle comes because we had previously laid siege to the shrine. We are all wise. The difference between persons is not in wisdom but in art. . . . Perhaps, if we should meet Shakespeare, we should not be conscious of any steep inferiority; no: but of a great equality—only that he possessed a strange skill of using, of classifying his facts, which we lacked.

*   *   *

By Otis M. Walter, Professor of Rhetorical Theory at the University of Pittsburgh in his Abstract of his article, "Creativity and the Rules of Rhetoric," in *The Journal of Creative Behavior,* Volume I, Number 4, Fall, 1967:

The rules of rhetoric do not incorporate the conditions necessary for creativity, and hence some of these rules may stifle. Creativity, however, seems to follow a vague pattern involving relatively long, and sometimes laborious sub-steps that must be carefully executed if the final product is to be of worth. The speaker or writer must undergo a preparation period, involving both direct preparation and indirect preparation. Usually, he will also experience a plateau period. The moment of insight may occur suddenly, and often while he is indulging in relaxing activity. The period of refining, which is necessary to make the final product perceptibly of merit involves checking, proving and stating the insight. These processes do not lead inevitably to creativity, and some of them may be repeated more than others; nevertheless, speakers and writers may be more creative by intentionally trying to follow them.

*   *   *

The plan given in the Preface of the syllabus parallels the four processes Walter mentions. They are indicated in Section 12 of the Syllabus which follows. These are in brief:

1. The Preparation Process
2. The Plateau Period
3. The Moment of Insight
4. The Period of Refining—the hours of researching which follow this work and culminate in your final exam.

XII

Showing Reading and Writing Ability, Library Usage and Recognizing Relationships of Ideas

READING (Note: This unit will require three or four weeks.)

Preparing for this unit, the teacher should read "Creativity and the Rules of Rhetoric" referred to in the Introduction to this Syllabus and there given in Abstract by the author of the article. If available, the entire article should be read. The students should be told that they are beginning work which will lead directly to the final examination writing, which is the rough draft of the body of their research paper based on "an idea of your own" as indicated in the "Preface, To the Student," page 7, of *America Is People and Ideas*.

Read and re-read pages 20 to 28 of the text to understand how the student should expect to recognize his own mind at work. Prepare at teacher-designated intervals the four paragraphs required below. These are to be passed in and held uncorrected but read by the teacher so that he may discover the type of mechanical error the students are still making and which need class discussion to erase. When the paragraphs are completed and "cold," they will be returned for the student to proofread and determine which is the best he has written. The "best" paragraph will be copied over and stapled to the top of all the paragraphs which are now ready for grading. The top paper will now be carefully graded and, if the teacher, by glancing at the other paragraphs, believes the student has not recognized his "best" work, additional credit will be deducted.

WRITING

In this unit of work the four "sub-processes" which Walter outlines in his "Creativity and the Rules of Rhetoric" should be brought to the students' attention so that they may realize how creative the work they are now doing is, and that each experience they will have from now to the end of the term will parallel one of Walter's four "sub-processes."

"The Preparation Process" by paragraphs A and B
"The Plateau Period" by paragraph C
"The Moment of Insight" by paragraph D
"The Period of Refining" by the hours of research work which follows these paragraphs and culminates with the final examination, or perhaps not even there.

The following Reading and Writing directions refer to each of the paragraphs, A to D, to be prepared for this unit.

A   Paragraph A is based on "Topics for Library Researching," pages 200 to 202, and is the Preparation Process.

READING

Using the topic assigned you by the teacher (it is very likely that you will not be at all interested in or know anything about the topic you are assigned), go to the library to find factual information on which you will take careful notes. If your library has a copying machine, it is permissible for you to mechanically copy the information you need. Contribute this information, in whatever form your teacher requests, to the class folder which the teacher will now make available to you by placing it on Reserve in the library or providing some other opportunity for you to read the class papers by yourself. (Some teachers may prefer to have each student read his library-discovered material aloud in class, but it is generally better for the student to do the reading at his own convenience and his own ability to concentrate so that he may be better preparing himself for the writing experience which follows this reading work.)

WRITING

AS YOU READ the several articles on the library reserve shelf for your class, BE AWARE of your MIND IN ACTION and know that the writing you are required to do will verbalize these thoughts in a well-developed paragraph. Be absolutely honest with yourself in expressing your thoughts, however unflattering they may be toward this assignment. Don't be surprised if your emotions change as you do your reading. Plan to use all or only certain reading information, whichever accords with your thoughts. The topic sentence you select might well have these words in it: Emotions, Frustrations, Interest, Curiosity. Pass the paragraph in to the teacher knowing that she will read it but that you will be expected to do your own Proofreading later on to prove your gain in mechanical ability.

B   Paragraph B is based on newspaper reading using teacher-prepared periodicals' clippings and the student's own collection.

READING

Read at your ease, and according to your curiosity and interests, the newspaper and magazine clippings prepared in file folders which your teacher has made available to you. Begin to realize that the periodicals' clippings which both you and your teacher have accumulated carry forward into the present and future the articles on which you and your classmates based your paragraph A reading and writing. Read these clippings, also, knowing that you, as an American citizen, are discovering the variety of topics the liberally educated man must be familiar with; and constantly realize the relationships among items to your personal interests.

Note that the topics Conservation and Ornithology listed on page 201 are becoming more and more in the news as dramatic and concerned problems which American youth today must be prepared to cope with. Sheer numbers inheriting the earth and treating natural resources carelessly may prove the truth of Antonia Maury's statement on page 25, even before the hundred years she gives us, if we continue to abuse the soil as we have in the past.

WRITING

Paragraph B should now have as its topic sentence some variation of the following ideas: "Areas of study today are so necessary, so diversified, and so constantly being added to that a student must depend upon his reading of the periodicals to keep abreast of the times in almost every discipline." "Education never ends." "The educated man will always be a reading man." "Conservation is literally 'man learning to serve with nature.'"

C   Paragraph C is based on some A-V tape requiring careful listening! This is the Plateau Period.

READING

Listen attentively to the tape your teacher plays for you. Take careful notes and be aware of your own thoughts which may be weighing what you hear. The tape must challenge the student to think of himself as an alive, active citizen. At Palm Beach Junior College the speech given at the dedication of AUTEC (Atlantic Underwater Test and Evaluating Center) is used because it enumerates the areas of study and research which young Americans should be pursuing today. Whatever tape is used, the student must recall his first A-V experience this term in being aware of his own thoughts while watching or listening to a speech. This assignment should be considerably easier for him and he should appreciate his growth as a student.

WRITING

Paragraph C will have a topic sentence consistent with the A-V material used and will reflect the student's personal reaction to what he has heard or seen. In regard to the AUTEC tape, the topic sentence could be "Florida may become the hub of Inner Space, Oceanography, in the future."

D   Paragraph D describes "the Moment of Insight" and is based on "A Practical Example of Recognized Relationships of Ideas," page 20.

READING

Preparation for paragraph D requires re-reading of pages 20 to 28 and a conscious awareness that the student has been led to be aware of his own ideas as they have come to him, often in the midst of seemingly unrelated ideas. The Emerson quotation on page 204 should be reread. The student should be consciously looking forward to "the moment, and unannounced, [when] the truth appears." He should recognize, too, that "the oracle comes because we had previously laid siege to the shrine."

WRITING

Paragraph D will be written on the experience you had arriving at the subject you now plan to pursue in your final research work. You may well have changed your ideas many times before the right idea strikes you. It is hoped it has come to you as the "moment of insight" which Walter refers to and which Emerson encourages you to anticipate. This will be the general area for your study and your further library researching; now much reading and thinking will allow you to narrow down your work to your actual thesis Idea. You will also be aware that you are entering on Walter's fourth and final stage of creativity as you "refine" your work.

CONCLUSION OF SECTION XII

Completion of Section 12 and review of all Mechanical Principles. If possible, the instructor should use the Opaque Projector to call to the student's attention the errors in mechanics which they are still making. Pass all the paragraphs back for completion of Section 12.

PROOFREADING

When the teacher returns paragraphs A, B, C, and D, proofread them and determine which, in the light of the grammar and punctuation review you have just had, is your best paragraph. Rewrite this paragraph and staple it to the top of the paragraphs done in this section and pass it in for severe correcting. Be aware of the relative ease with which you wrote the latter paragraphs compared with the first one.

PREPARING THE FORMAL PAPER

This final section of the text gives practical information and examples of the mechanics of library reference work. It includes:

1. Bibliography cards which indicate the necessary information to obtain when taking notes in the library on books and/or magazines. The cards illustrate the differences between a footnote reference and a bibliography listing for books and magazines.

   CAUTION: Be sure to fill in every possible blank in the cards to save having to return to the library for information necessary to document your notes when you decide to use them in your formal paper. Write on only one side of the cards on which you take notes from your reading.

2. A shadow sheet to be used under each page of your final draft to insure proper margins, etc.
3. A reference page called Information for Using Reference Cards.
4. A classroom sample of footnoting following the directions on the Information sheet.
5. A scholarly example of writing based on the Colloquium (Latin for conversation), a conference, sponsored by the Hazen Foundation.

INFORMATION FOR USING RESEARCHING FORMS
Bibliography and Footnote Cards—
for *BOOKS* and *PERIODICALS*

Follow directions printed on the cards when you type up your bibliography. Note carefully the punctuation called for on the card. Single space the bibliography entries and double space between the entries. For the footnotes be sure you plan ahead, as you write each sheet, so that you will have room for each footnote needed on the specific page and allow for the bottom one-inch margin. Follow directions on the card for footnote arrangement and punctuation. Single space the footnote and double space between the footnotes. Use *Ibid.* and the *op cit.* type of reference (author and page) whenever possible. If you have an unusual item to footnote and enter in your bibliography, refer to one of the several manuals available to you in the reserve library. Many disciplines (subjects) require their own style manual. Be prepared to obtain one if necessary.

Shadow Sheet Directions

Use this sheet to provide the margins you must follow on different pages. Place the sheet under your working page. General directions are as follows:

1. Title Page. Use the three blocks or lines for your material and center each line between the proper side margins.

2. Thesis Statement and Outline Page. Head this page "Outline" placing the word on the 1½"-top margin line. Begin the thesis statement at the left margin and type or write single-spaced. Double space before the outline proper. Begin item 1 at the left margin. This may be your brief Introduction or, if you wish, you may write the Introduction as a separate unit before you begin the first item in your outline. In this case double space between the Introduction and 1. Follow the necessary procedure of indenting according to the items and sub-items in your outline. Handle the final item, Conclusion, so that it corresponds with the manner in which you wrote the Introduction. Single space all items in the Introduction.

3. First Page. Write the title so that you have the full 1½" margin above your writing. Do not use a page number on this page. Begin the text of your paper on the third line below the title. Double space the body of your paper or write on every other line. Write over to the right margin but not beyond it so that you have a definite one-inch margin.

4. Second and all other pages will have the page number centered between the margins and half an inch down from the top. Have one-inch margin above your writing at the top of all pages from here on.

5. Within the paper, if you quote an extended passage, indent these lines an extra half inch at left and right, and single space. In this event, do not use quotation marks.

6. Place all footnote numbers at the end of the borrowed material and raise the footnote numbers half a space. Align the number at the beginning of the footnote.

7. Bibliography page. Handle this page as you do the first page; i.e., write the word "Bibliography" so that you have the 1½" margin above the word. Begin the first entry at the left margin. Single space entries and double space between items.

No.   BIBLIOGRAPHY **(PERIODICALS)**

Indent five (5) spaces
after first line

Subject ____

Author (last name first)   Other Authors (first name first)   Title

of the article   Source (underlined)

Volume   month   day   year   Page(s)

(Personal information--library where found, etc.)

* *

at five (5) spaces
paragraph form

No.   FOOTNOTE

Author (first name first)   Other Authors (same)   Title

of the article   Source

Volume   Month

Day   Year   , p. __________ .

No. Ibid., p. __________ .

* No. __________________   p. __________ .
  Last name of Author(s)

* Note: Your instructor may wish
  to vary this op.cit. reference.
  If so, be consistent in the change
  throughout the paper.

No.   BIBLIOGRAPHY (BOOKS)

Indent five (5) spaces
after first line

Subject

Author (last name first)   Other Authors (first name first)   Title

of the book (underlined)   Volume   Place of

Publication   Publisher   year

(Personal information -- library found, etc.)

* *

No.   FOOTNOTE

Indent five (5) spaces
for paragraph form

Author (first name first)   Other Authors (same)   Title

of the Book (underlined)   Volume   Place of

Publication   Publisher

Year   ) , p. ______
                              Page(s)

            No. Ibid., p. ______
            (underlined)   Page(s)

      * No. ________________ p. ______ .
            Last name of author(s)   Page(s)

*Note: Your instructor may wish
to vary this op. cit. reference.
If so, be consistent in the change
throughout your paper.

A SAMPLE STUDENT RESEARCH PAPER

(Developed as a classroom project, this sample paper is the result of student contributions of facts and references in the classroom where they were combined in this essay.)

MATTHEW FONTAINE MAURY, OCEANOGRAPER

The outstanding feature of the period of history in which we live is the profusion of technical marvels made possible by science. So accustomed are we to these inventions that it is nearly impossible to surprise us. In the year 1960, one of the events with which the mass media impressed the public was the awesome journey in August of the atomic submarine the *Seadragon* under the icebergs from Baffin Bay to the Bering Sea.[1]

This journey is only one of many developments resulting from the rapid expansion of the science of oceanography, to which the International Geophysical Year contributed a great deal.[2] For example, one may read the interesting reports of the IGY findings in *Life* and other magazines.[3] The tragic loss of life on board the submarine *Thresher* on April 10, 1963, was the cause of the Navy's three-stage plan set up the same year for study of the sea, in the hope of preventing more accidents due to ignorance of the ocean depths.[4] A growing number of oceanographic research centers witness to the growing interest in exploring inner space, an interest that is rivaling our interest in outer space. The work begun on Project Mo-Hole[5] in the Pacific Ocean and the studies at Wood's Hole Oceanographic Institution on Cape Cod, Massachusetts,[6] are very interesting examples of such activities.

---

1. Louise Davis, "Pathfinder of the Seas: a Three-Part Series," *The Nashville Tennessean Magazine*, XXI (Sept. 25, 1960), p. 89.

2. Dorothy Myers Peed, *America Is People and Ideas* (New York: Exposition Press, 1966), p. 111.

3. *Ibid.*

4. *Miami Herald*, an editorial (July 10, 1963), p. 3A.

5. Peed, p. 110.

6. Peed, p. 109.

In 1963 Florida Atlantic University, in Boca Raton, likewise planned to set up a research center (now accomplished), a multimillion-dollar project to cover study over a period of ten years.[7] In Mystic, Connecticut, there is a museum based on whaling,[8] an institution that can be important in adding knowledge in the field of oceanography, since through the study of the life and habits of the whale much can be learned about the laws that operate in the sea.[9] Now researchers are considering using sharks also for this purpose. They think they can fasten on the dorsal fin a "Pinger" whose sound can be picked up by underwater tracking gear so that the shark's movements can be recorded.[10]

This greatly increased activity in the fascinating exploration of inner space is triggered by a growing realization of all that oceanography has meant and may mean in the future to the human race. Its importance lies not only in its usefulness in providing adequate defense for our shores, but in its contribution to all areas of life affected by science, government, and industry. Its possibilities are practically unlimited as a source of minerals and new kinds of food.[11]

Do we tend to forget the past in all this brilliant accomplishment in the present and high hopes for the future? Do we fail to lose sight of what we owe to the pioneers without whose "blood, sweat and tears" these achievements would have been impossible? After all, does real value lie in *things*, like submarines, minerals, and food—even knowledge itself? or does it lie in the people who are the givers of things, and in ourselves as potential givers inspired by those great lives?

Did you ever hear, before reading *America Is People and Ideas*, of the pioneer oceanographer, Matthew Fontaine Maury? Was he included in your history books? Probably not, and why

---

7. An editorial, *Miami Herald*, p. 3A.
8. Peed, p. 99.
9. Davis, p. 99.
10. Peed, p. 100.
11. Hon. James H. Wakelin, Jr., An editorial, *Data*, CI (May, 1963), p. 9.

not? Is it possible that history sometimes ignores those most worthy of acclaim? At least one writer, upon reading of the *Seadragon's* exploit, remembered the man who first found the whale's route that the *Seadragon* followed, and honored him in a glowing account of his life's achievements.[12] Surely these accomplishments warrant for this real genius, Matthew Fontaine Maury, a a prominent place among the great names of American history.

BIBLIOGRAPHY

Davis, Louise. "Pathfinder of the Seas: a Three-Part Series," *The Tennesean,* XXI (Sept. 25, 1960), p. 89.

Miami Herald. An editorial (July 10, 1963), p. 3A.

Peed, Dorothy Myers. *America Is People and Ideas* (New York: Exposition Press, 1966), p. 111.

Wakelin, Jr., Hon. James H. An editorial in *Data,* CI (May, 1963), p. 9.

A SAMPLE OF A SCHOLARLY PAPER

The following essay is the third section of a report of Colloquium III held at Bellagio, Italy, 1972, by the Hazen Foundation. The sixteen participants in the Colloquium came from the four corners of the world. An excerpt from the preface of the full report entitled "Reconstituting the Human Community" reads as follows:

> We, the undersigned, after an intensive final week of dialogue at Bellagio, Italy, in Colloquium III of Cultural Relations for the Future, want to share the following convictions and urgent recommendations with all who are interested in the improvement of cultural relations in our time. . . .
>
> We are aware of a growing network of individuals concerned with the improvement of long-term cultural relations among peoples and countries who wish to transcend the barriers—political, military or ideological—which often distort or handicap the ful-

---

12. Davis, p. 89.

fillment of human relationships. At the conclusion of our deliberations we have agreed to share our thoughts and convictions through a series of publications, to continue our inquiries in various specific ways through the Study Groups and in new regional intergroup programs and to endeavor to create channels of communication with other concerned individuals and groups.

Although the essay below does not have a thesis statement in the sense that we have discussed them under complex sentences, this sentence from another section of the report can serve as the thesis:

"Rich and poor nations alike face the problem of helping to restore and build a humane society, for we are a divided world, torn by factionalism, civil strife and deep national, ethnic, tribal and ideological divisions."

THE CULTURAL SEARCH FOR MEANING:
MAN, YOUTH AND VALUES*

A.   The forces that shape the context for cultural relations, and the emerging role and opportunities of Asians and Africans therein, raise fundamental questions of values and meaning. Young people across the world are looking for alternatives and seek deeper understandings of the nature of man and society. They are open to imaginative insights that might lead to a more humane future. In the world in which we live, one of the most valuable and promising forms of cultural exchange is to increase the range of human interests and skills that shape the life-style of a whole civilization. These concerns go to the basic factors that determine what each civilization is and can become, and therefore, are of primary and continuing importance, not to be neglected until economic development and environmental problems have been "solved." Cultural relations widen the range in which man can live his life, including working out the relationships of means and ends, technology and social purpose and one set of cultural goals to another. In preparing for the future, it is vital to see

---

*Used by permission of the Hazen Foundation, 400 Prospect Street, New Haven, Connecticut 06511.

cultural exchange as a means of broadening the area of choice and widening the fund of human experience, thus making it possible to build a new and happier and more civilized life.

Redefinition of the nature of man

B. It is important to identify the first part of this topic as man, and not as "citizen" or "world citizen" or "economic man," but boldly and unequivocally as man, because there is more at stake than man's position as an element in political restructuring of the world or in relation to his obligations as a citizen. The problem we are all facing is the redefinition of the concept of man as the whole man. It has become an urgent problem because of a new plasticity that the concept of man has gained in recent and emerging cultural relationships, but also in the light of advances of science, including genetic intervention of various kinds, organ transplants and so-called mind-expanding or memory-building drugs. They all reopen the question of how we define man. There is also a whole range of problems opened by developments in the biological and other sciences. It is not enough to say that future civilization should be man-oriented or man-centered. It is also necessary to inquire into the "quality" of the man of the future and also that this quality be such that it has meaning and is a source of motivation. Man is man to the extent that he wants to be more than he is to transcend himself, and to be certain that this quality will indeed insure survival and progress. The danger is that he may become hypnotized by self-love and thereby fall prey to the dangers of pride and arrogance. Impending developments cannot be truly beneficial unless men are able to overcome or channel their egoism, vanity and aggressiveness and nourish characteristics of openness and humility, developing a readiness to concede and to share. These qualities grow out of a deep faith in the dignity of the human person and an alert consciousness of and respect and concern for "the other" (whether an individual or a group). This concern for the other, this transcendence of self, whether that "self" be an individual, nation, class, race or creed, is, we venture to affirm, the essence of morality. Without such morality, not only will the human condition remain highly precarious, but the needed universalism, even if achieved, will prove to be impotent and without content and the desired humanism will bring more evil than good.

C. Still another dimension in which man will have to seek redefinition is in terms of the crowded world in which he will have to live. Until the present, his preoccupation has been with freedom as the essential condition for the flowering of his potential. That may not any longer be the central problem for him, although we are fully aware of restrictions on freedom in most societies. Man's individual and human rights are still too often impaired and we must all keep striving for the creation of those conditions that improve the conditions under which he lives. However, another focus is emerging, involving the restraints that men have to put on themselves to live in a more crowded world. The population crisis is creating moral problems of tremendous complexity, such as abortion, birth control and the need for a more rational and spatial distribution of population, focusing on the balance between individual human rights and the collective survival needs of a nation or community. Thus, the problem of human rights and freedom entails a search for an appropriate balance between individual human rights and the social obligations essential for man if he is to live in a civilized manner with more neighbors than his ancestors knew. His personal living space is becoming severely limited. In this connection, Japan is an example of a civilization that for centuries has responded to extreme crowding on a few islands and which has, as a result, evolved a social system giving priority to the needs of community life. In many and diverse situations what is most needed is more self-knowledge, more about what we can expect in the new crowded world so we may identify emerging problems before they become critical and we are forced to react in panic.

D. Another aspect of the redefinition of man's concept of himself is the need for greater sobriety in viewing the place of material goods. In the rich countries ecological necessities will force a slowing down of the growth rate, new consumption patterns, new concepts of happiness and the good life and a reexamination of basic drives. Some very basic cultural questions are involved and can lead to new images of man in society, involving renewed stress on participation with accountability. We will become acutely aware, once again, of the urgency of various concepts of coexistence, the ways of resolving conflicts and the rebirth of the notion of public responsibility.

E. These considerations raise questions about the appropriate role of science and technology or, more precisely, of man's use of them. While science and scientific knowledge are in themselves a product of man's quest and achievement, there remains a problem of the relevance of new knowledge to the urgent problems of the world and of society. A strong case can be made for a redirection of some of the resources that are available to science and the scholarly world toward an attack on international poverty, overpopulation and other emerging problems. This will inevitably mean a reduction in the amounts available for the creation of technologies of convenience for the saturated markets of rich countries, which spill over into developing urban areas around the world. The test will come in the ability of the rich countries to respond to the challenge.

F. Finally, man has to redefine his relationship to society and to art. Part of the problem is the rediscovery or identification of patterns for happiness and the good life. Art has perennial and enduring relevance, for aesthetic expression is a basic human need. Furthermore, art expresses the convictions and commitments of Man. Perhaps we have to look for a revitalization of the concept of art in terms of community life, rather than as exclusively an expression of individual self-consciousness. In the emerging world order, in which fuller and more rewarding community living in both cities and rural areas will be achieved, it is important from the outset to consider ways in which men can express themselves aesthetically in community life. In this connection it is important to recall that many of the traditional arts of Asian and African peoples are activities in which a whole community participates. This is an area for study, experimentation and innovation which may yield large benefits, not only in those areas, but in the affluent countries as well.

The contribution of youth

G. Again and again in our inquiries, we have found ourselves absorbed with the concerns and interests, the aspirations and frustrations of youth in whatever situation they find themselves. Here we do not address ourselves to "youth" as such because our primary concern is with new ideas, perspectives and problems which all will face in a world where the whole population is steadily getting younger. In a country like Indonesia, for instance, more than half of the population is below nineteen years of age, and in the United States thirty million are between eighteen and twenty-five. The World Bank now reports the median age world-wide is seventeen years. Under these circumstances, it is not possible to speak with detachment of "youth" as a rather minor problem apart. Contemporary youth are in a particularly strategic situation since they will be most affected by future developments and inevitably will be involved in cultural relations.

H. As a recent United Nations study has pointed out: "There is a growing sense of unity among young people, a feeling of world solidarity and a sense of common responsibility to achieve peace. Youth of the world is seeking a universal identity. This is a new kind of population, more resilient and adaptable than their elders, ready for change, open to new ideas. Youth of the world will soon predominate in world affairs." Thus we must recognize and encourage thoughtful young people to build more networks of relationships nationally, intra-regionally and inter-regionally. The problems of youth are our problems and we must think of them in terms of the totality of our communities and our societies.

I. A central problem in cultural relations for the future is the need to reconsider and facilitate the role of young people in the creation of a new and different world. This may mean institutional changes, making it possible for younger people to assume greater responsibility earlier in life. It may mean establishing educational methods to enable youth to learn certain essential things more quickly and to prepare for a career or careers more effectively than under traditional educational systems. It may mean the development of new patterns of work and learning and different career perspectives in business, government or education. And these are but a few of the ways in which urgent efforts must be made to harness and channel the creative and dynamic social energy of youth.

J. Thus new concepts of the future and new patterns of work will have to be worked out. The young must participate and share responsibility. This will require tremendous institutional change in all societies. But it does not mean that the older generation should abdicate its responsibilities. They ought never hold back suggestions, ideas or solutions drawn from their deeper knowledge of history and broader experience. The older generation owes it to youth, as to itself, to fight for its ideas and principles and in no way deprive youth of the right and the privilege, in return, of fighting for its ideas. An Asian proverb states, "It is a terrible thing to have a reasonable father!" It is only in struggle that the identity of youth can be delineated and their ideas and notions hardened and refined into useful concepts. Thus one cannot speak helpfully about youth and the cultural changes in society that will be essential for the future unless he speaks of both generations, the older and the younger. Their relationship will vary within each civilization and society. A great deal of thinking and searching is essential on the part of young and old, and especially of both together.

Implication of values differentials

K. One aspect of this search will be a working through of new and emergent ethical problems and the search for a new ethics of survival. In fact, when man faces the future he in reality faces himself; so the problem is to help devise the instrumentalities that will make this search feasible. We shall have to think in new directions, not only on broad philosophical problems but about hard specifics such as the writing of children's books (which shape values), and about the operational and functional values which will enhance the survival capacities of man. We must think about new rituals, and new forms of celebration of those values that will be functional in the future. These are some of the contours of this important subject that bespeak urgent and continuing consideration.

L. The problem is very real and crucial. It is close to the heart of any program for the improvement of cultural relations in the future. It arises because of the values differential in the world. The value systems of the young, insofar as they have an integrated and overall system, are reactions to their own personal and societal problems. These reactions are broadly of two types: tending either toward social activism in responses ranging from blind violence to experimental and alternative types of social organization; or to religious and spiritual experiences, with or without drugs. Youth in the developing nations are to a considerable degree social activists in reacting to their own societal situation represented by inequality, poverty and backwardness. At the same time, the values of many youth in the developing nations represent personal philosophies that have been abandoned elsewhere, particularly as they relate to the inner world.

M. What then is the problem? And what means should be used to link up the potential for social change and transformation in the rich and the poor countries seen through the eyes of the idealistic young? Simple exchange is probably not the answer because it will only emphasize the distance between the rich and the poor. The hope that there will be a common revolution that will link them up in a kind of natural fashion is also an illusion because there is little revolutionary potential among young people in the West. The latter are limited by an essentially particularistic and anarchistic concept of society. Their reaction to the over-organization and over-bureaucratization of modern society is to form themselves into spontaneous small groups that appear and disappear according to needs. This prevents continuing organization for recurrent needs. What is possible is less a restructuring of society than a revolutionary dissolution of organized society through increased chaos, both in the rich and the poor countries.

N. What is needed therefore is not simply increasing contact and exchange, but rather some unifying vision of the human person and of the world that gives proper place to the flight into the inner world linking up with the religious experiences of the past—and to search for new societal forms, grounded both in experience and imagination. A world vision combining these two perspectives could provide a grand design for cultural relations for the future. How is this going to come about? The first requirement is a clear definition of the need—a unifying vision worked out by individuals and groups and modelled to fit their particular situations. For this the task is not so much to increase contact but to find exceptional and creative individuals, wherever located, who have the ability to see new relationships. This calls less for a formal organization and more for searching out extraordinary individuals wherever they can be found, finding ways to assist them, bringing them into touch with one another and encouraging them to foster creative impulses, rather than stifling them in the name of the *status quo*.

O.   One element of this problem is the danger that communication across national boundaries among those who seek new approaches and new answers might be complicated by a phase differential of their cultures. A very important, even crucial, aspect of cultural relations in the future is to find ways of coping with this problem. Simple increase in contacts by number or intensity will not be sufficient. Communications of much greater intensity and longer duration are necessary—and for this various new or rediscovered small institutions of an Ashram sort, as recommended strongly by the Southeast Asian Study Group, deserve very serious attention and testing.

P.   Another aspect of this situation is the increased antagonism between governments or adminstrators and the younger generation, particularly in parts of the world where dissent is feared and tolerance limited. The irony and tragedy of this is that it occurs at a time when social change is desperately needed and when the resources of idealistic and courageous youth are at a high peak. Their contributions should be welcomed and encouraged, and ways discovered to bring them into the decision-making and development planning of the future.

Q.   The urgent need, then, is for a higher vision, a clearer scale of values and a fresh sense of what is worth living and dying for. We would encourage individuals and concerned groups to seek ways to synthesize those fragmentary social and ethical impulses that are appearing in the world into a single, unifying world outlook—a kind of scenario of hope, but a scenario within the horizon of feasibility that could give direction and purpose to the striving of both young and old to find their place in the future world order. Such a scenario would have to include and interrelate guidelines for understanding such issues as the conditions and maintenance of peace, disarmament, the dividends of peace, a new ecological balance, the concept of social or distributive justice nationally and internationally and a political order dealing more relevantly with the distribution and utilization of raw materials. It would be a blueprint with a difference for it would provide for flexibility and growth.